The Feedback Process

Transforming Feedback for Professional Learning

By Joellen Killion

THE PROFESSIONAL LEARNING ASSOCIATION

Learning Forward
504 S. Locust St.
Oxford, OH 45056
800-727-7288
Fax: 513-523-0638
Email: office@learningforward.org
www.learningforward.org

The Feedback Process:
Transforming Feedback
for Professional Learning
By Joellen Killion

Editor: Joyce Pollard
Copy editor: Tracy Crow
Designer: Jane Thurmond
Photo credits: Thinkstock

Printed in the United States of America
Item B591

ISBN: 978-0-9903158-4-1

Contents

Acknowledgements

Many people contributed to this work. I want to thank Stephanie Hirsh who urged me to write this book, offered to write it with me, supported me with encouragement, prodding when necessary, and reminded me about the significance of feedback in educators' professional learning.

Tracy Crow listened to me as I struggled with terms and language. She encouraged me to continue to push through my frustration with traditional views of feedback. She opened the floodgates by giving me permission to abandon the use of *giver* and *receiver* that connote a view of feedback inconsistent with mine.

The participants in my sessions on feedback at the 2014 Teaching and Learning Conference sponsored annually by the University of Kansas Center for Research on Learning's Instructional Coaching program once again served as my thinking partners and provided me a forum to test out ideas. Without hesitation, they told me which ideas worked and which didn't, questioned some, and offered insightful suggestions about others. I am grateful for coaches who are willing learners and learner partners.

Each of the people below acted as my learning partner in this work and through other initiatives. They responded to my request for their most pressing questions about feedback. They offered ideas and suggestions to guide and organize my thinking and identify what was missing. Pages of their ideas stayed close at hand for frequent reference. Some read earlier versions of the book and suggested revisions. Each of them has a unique contribution to the ideas within the book. I am grateful for their perspectives, questions, ideas, and suggestions.

Jennifer Abrams	Cindy Harrison
Denny Berry	Saundra Hamon
Chris Bryan	Lindsey Kauserud
Lisa Casto	Nikki Golar Moulton
Heather Clifton	Linda Munger
Amy Colton	Kay Psencik
Ann Delehant	Dyan Smiley
Victoria Duff	DeNelle West

So many people offered encouragement and ideas in conversations as I was planning and writing this book. Their questions and ideas stimulated me to consider and reconsider many aspects of this book.

A writer benefits from a strong editor. An editor becomes the learning partner described in this book, someone who clarifies, reflects, queries, and probes another's thinking to make sense of the words on the page. This is my experience with Joyce Pollard who has been at my side for over three years as my learning partner and editor. She has the unique capacity to listen to complex ideas and sort them out so they can be communicated clearly. As a long-time specialist in communication, she understands how the reader's experience contributes to meaning of text and uses that expertise to facilitate the text's construction to support the reader.

A book's design influences its readability and usefulness. Not every book is designed to engage the reader and support the reading experience. A designer's skillfulness and artistry influence people's willingness to open the cover and facilitate the reading experience. Jane Thurmond creates page designs, text layout, and graphics that helped both the author and editor throughout the creative process. She uses the page to clarify, organize, and illustrate ideas within the text.

The constant support and patient ear of Terry Killion made this book possible. He brought me coffee, listened to me, allowed me space for focused work, and never complained. He is what makes my life possible and has been my feedback practice partner for more than 40 years.

Foreword

Like everyone else, my life has been enriched by feedback. My parents gave me feedback on how to walk through the complexities of life on earth. My teachers gave me feedback on how to learn. My students' blank stares gave me feedback on how to be a better teacher. Teachers' evaluation forms from workshops gave me feedback on how to be a better professional developer. Professional colleagues, like Joellen Killion, gave me feedback that has helped me be a better researcher, writer, and thinker.

Joellen has been my friend and colleague for more than a decade, and she has been the best kind of friend — the kind who challenges my thinking and helps me learn more. Joellen and I share a deep commitment to doing what it takes for all children and teachers to succeed, but we sometimes disagree on the best strategies for achieving that goal. The result of our differences, speaking only for me, is that Joellen's candor and insight help me see more and think deeper. She has had the same impact on me with this timely, important book, *The Feedback Process: Transforming Feedback for Professional Learning.*

In this scholarly, comprehensive, and pioneering book about feedback Joellen Killion asserts that feedback is a process and not a product. Thus, she puts the focus of feedback, in my opinion, where it should be, on learning. What is critical with feedback is whether or not it produces growth and learning. In other words, skillfully crafted feedback that doesn't prompt growth or learning is no better than poorly crafted feedback that doesn't lead to change — what matters is growth, learning, and change.

Feedback, Joellen explains, can come from at least three different sources and occur in at least nine different types. These are all useful distinctions. But most important is Joellen's point that the critical variable separating good feedback from poor feedback is what happens in the learner's head rather than the feedback-giver's head. We need to rethink feedback. Rather than thinking of it as what happens when knowledgeable people impart their wisdom to less knowledgeable people, we need to think of feedback as being a part of a learning partnership that helps learners construct new and better understandings of how they do what they do.

We can learn about what a learning partnership is by considering what it is not. I spoke with an assistant principal from the South who was in the first year of his position, and he told me about the difficulties he was facing as he tried to implement his district's teacher evaluation model. "The way I see it," he said, "if the teacher doesn't cry or doesn't get angry, it's a good feedback session." A coach from the Pacific Northwest told me that she watched her principal write his walk-through feedback for a teacher on a sticky note **before** he watched the teacher's lesson. Then he gave the note to her as he left. He'd written, "You are a breath of fresh air." Both examples set a pretty low bar for feedback.

In the two examples above, feedback is for compliance, not learning. Feedback is a task to be checked off a list — even if it has no impact. Feedback of this sort is something done to other people, simply because it has to be done. A better idea is a learning partnership, one where teacher and learning partner (who might be a principal, coach, or peer) wrestle with ideas together.

A learning partnership is a different kind of conversation, one where both partners bring their brains and hearts to the conversation. In a learning partnership both partners see each other as people they trust, whose thoughts and voice matter. When we are in a learning partnership, we engage in what I refer to as a better conversation — one that makes both of us better. In a learning partnership we are not trying to get the other person to "buy-in" to our view of things, we are collaborating with each other to come up with a better understanding, or a better strategy, or a better way forward.

These might sound like very theoretical concepts, and readers would be right to say, "This all sounds great, but how do I do it?" And this is the beauty of this book: Joellen Killion provides us with clear definitions, guidelines, reflection forms, and strategies to help anyone get better at giving and receiving feedback. Furthermore, *The Feedback Process: Transforming Feedback for Professional Learning* offers a model for feedback that is precise but also adaptive. A one-size-fits-all model will not work for something as complex as teaching, but this is a model, grounded in research, that can be adapted to meet the unique needs of individual educators (teachers, coaches, and principals) and their schools and classrooms.

Joellen also reminds us that too often policymakers have an understanding of feedback as something that is a technical product rather than an adaptive process. She urges us, in fact, to give our policymakers some feedback — namely, they need to rethink their understanding of feedback and recognize it as a professional partnership that produces learning rather than simply something that has to be done.

Perhaps the best way we can promote such a new understanding is by taking Joellen's ideas to heart, both in the way we give and receive feedback. This is an extremely important task to take on. I am convinced that a fulfilling life is impossible without learning, and learning is impossible without feedback. It is not an exaggeration, then, to say that becoming better at feedback will help us have a better life. Truly, feedback is that important. This book can help anyone get much better at giving and receiving it.

— Jim Knight
*University of Kansas Center
for Research on Learning*

Introduction

Feedback enriches learning. Yet not all feedback has the same effect on the learning process. Consider the following cases about two different uses of feedback in education.

Case A

Shantelle is a fifth-year teacher and grade-level chair. In the previous school year's annual performance review, her supervisor noted that she is an accomplished teacher, yet her students and other 5th-graders at the school were not progressing in math at the same rate as other students across the district. He recommended that the team's professional goal be to improve student performance through formative assessments, data analysis, and adjustments to instruction. She agreed that the goal would help the team uncover some of the challenges with student learning.

As the school year progresses, the team looks more closely at student data to identify gaps in student learning. They develop and implement common assessments and make adjustments in their math instructional practices and student learning tasks. They recognize and adjust evident gaps in their units and lessons.

In periodic reviews with her supervisor during the year, Shantelle brings student performance data for him to review. She shares data and the 5th-grade team's analysis from the grade-level common assessments. She also presents revised units and lessons with annotations about the adjustments the team made. Her supervisor comments that she is very committed to her goal; he names the indicators related to several areas in the teacher performance rubric, specifically in the area of planning, instruction, and professional responsibility; and expresses appreciation for her leadership within the 5th-grade team. He adds that the real indicator will be in student test results that are due at the end of June. He thanks her for bringing these data and says he looks forward to seeing the student test results as much as she does.

Case B

Jonathan is a second-year middle school principal who acknowledges that he has a lot to learn. His goal is to exhibit instructional leadership by being in classrooms daily and conducting weekly learning walks with teams of teachers focused on the instructional framework. He also meets frequently with teachers to talk about their professional goals or review student data; later, he makes time to visit team meetings to observe and provide feedback and support.

Each month he meets with his own supervisor to review his overall work, address challenges that he is grappling with, assess progress toward his goal, and examine data he is collecting about the effects of his work. In each meeting, Jonathan and his supervisor use the principal performance standards to ground their examination of his practice. The supervisor begins by asking Jonathan to cite both successes and opportunities emerging from his work during the past month. He probes Jonathan's analysis of his practice, asks him to cite data, and listens deeply. He asks Jonathan about his assumptions and beliefs, his decision-making process, and his feelings. He often invites Jonathan to put himself in the shoes of someone else and consider the effects of his actions through the eyes of another.

While they devote some time to a review of the past month, the larger part of the conversation focuses on what Jonathan is learning and how it will influence his future actions. A common phrase they use is *lessons learned* as they consider how Jonathan's past choices will influence his future actions.

During the nearly 60-minute conversation, Jonathan explores multiple perspectives, assesses his own practice, and formulates conclusions. Then, he begins to consider how he might adapt those conclusions if he applied them in different situations. He strives to examine the assumptions guiding his decisions and actions; he explores how his actions would affect teachers, families, students, and himself as a leader. The conversation is punctuated with periods of silence as Jonathan constructs a deeper understanding about what it means to be an instructional leader.

• • • • •

The previous situations share commonalities. They are a part of an annual performance appraisal system. They involve a supervisor and supervisee. They focus on performance goals with periodic opportunities to review progress toward the goals. Yet, they differ in how the supervisee and supervisor interact, their roles in each conversation, and the content and purpose of the conversation.

In the first scenario the supervisor remains in the supervisor role: He names the indicators of performance and provides general recognition and approval of Shantelle's effort. He does not go as far as rating or judging her performance, although the subtext might suggest that his approval is synonymous with a positive rating. Shantelle is the recipient of the supervisor's feedback. At the end of the conversation she has heard that he approves of and appreciates her efforts, and that the judgment of success depends on student results.

In the second case the supervisor probes to promote learning. Through the shape of the conversation, the topics addressed, the silences, and balance of looking backward as a springboard to future actions, the second case places Jonathan in the lead role. Jonathan takes an active role in the conversation by unpacking his own thinking with the supervisor facilitating the construction of new insights and lessons learned. As a partner in the learning process, the supervisor cultivates Jonathan's ability to engage in self-analysis and knowledge construction independently. Jonathan leaves the meeting with a deeper understanding of the concept of instructional leadership, awareness of his own practice, and awareness of how his behaviors influence others. He also leaves with greater capacity to engage in self-generated feedback and recognition that it is valued.

Learning-focused feedback differs from other forms of feedback in its content, purpose, and process. It requires the participants in feedback conversations to take on specific roles that may not be evident in other feedback conversations. A question frequently asked about feedback is, "How do you get people to use it?" This question demonstrates that the current approach to feedback is insufficient because it presents an imbalance in responsibility and roles. It suggests that those asking the question see themselves as the master and the recipient as a responder to their demands or expectations. Learning-focused feedback changes these dynamics. These fundamental differences distinguish learning-focused feedback from other types.

The Feedback Process: Transforming Feedback for Professional Learning guides learners and their learning partners in generating and using a feedback process that results in change. The premise of this book is that feedback is an integral component of the cycle of continuous improvement. When integrated into ongoing professional learning and sustained support, feedback is a process for strengthening educators' professional practice and achieving greater results. *The Feedback Process: Transforming Feedback for Professional Learning* strives to increase the frequency and quality of the feedback process so that it is continuous, self-generated, and future-focused. Ultimately, the feedback process becomes a routine part of ongoing professional practice rather than an occasional one-way judgment of performance delivered by an external source.

This book is for learners who work side-by-side with them throughout the learning process. It will guide learning partners, supervisors, coaches, content experts, professional learning facilitators, consultants, mentors, teacher leaders, peers, and others who support adults in the learning process to transform feedback from static information into a dynamic process that places the learner in the driver seat. It is useful for supervisors whose primary responsibility is to lead learning among those they supervise and for those who want to use the performance appraisal process to promote continuous growth in practice. Others who facilitate learning among professionals will also find the discussion of the feedback process relevant (and perhaps revelatory) to their work.

At this point, a caution is in order about what this book does not do: It does not offer a how-to guide on giving one-way feedback, choosing words carefully, or sandwiching corrections between positive comments. Readers seeking such information will want to explore other sources.

Instead, the chapters examine feedback as a constructivist process that engages learners with their partners in generating and deconstructing knowledge. Discussions in each chapter invite readers to examine their assumptions about feedback and their feedback practices by digging into their own understanding of feedback. At the end of each chapter, reflection questions invite readers to review the chapter content and explore feedback and its role in the learning process of professionals. Related resources and tools in each chapter guide the reader in examining various types of feedback, understanding how to apply the feedback process, and constructing new knowledge about the role of feedback in learning and change.

The Feedback Process: Transforming Feedback for Learning includes the following chapters:

CHAPTER 1 — Feedback Fundamentals

Explores rationale of the feedback process. In this chapter, readers will find common misconceptions of feedback and definitions of key terms that are associated with the view of feedback presented in this book.

CHAPTER 2 — Feedback Defined — and Redefined

Examines definitions of feedback within the research literature, provides a definition of a learning-focused feedback process, and distinguishes this book's view of feedback from other more commonly held views.

CHAPTER 3 — Attributes of an Effective Feedback Process

Identifies and describes 11 attributes of effective, learning-focused feedback processes.

CHAPTER 4 — Feedback Conditions

Describes the conditions necessary for effective feedback related to the actors in the process and the environment.

CHAPTER 5 — Types of Feedback

Describes a primary typology along a continuum of nine forms of feedback based on their context and purposes.

CHAPTER 6 — Feedback Process

Describes the learning-focused feedback process and several variations.

CHAPTER 7 — Feedback Evidence

Discusses data and evidence used in the feedback process.

CHAPTER 8 — System Feedback

Discusses a systems-thinking approach used in the feedback process.

CHAPTER 9 — Future of Learning-focused Feedback

Examines policy and practice implications for the new view of feedback.

Feedback Fundamentals

1

Readers consider the rationale for shifting to a learning-focused feedback process. Readers will:

- Debunk common misconceptions of feedback based on traditional notions about the purpose of feedback.
- Learn definitions of key terms used throughout this book: learner, learning partner, learning object, information, and knowledge.
- Examine reflection questions about experiences with feedback.

Different individuals and teams use the feedback process for different purposes. This chapter describes how those involved in the feedback process use it to achieve deep learning. Not all feedback, however, aligns with the major premises described in this book. Such misalignment occurs because those engaged in the feedback process have developed practices based on misconceptions about the types and purposes of feedback and have not considered alternatives to their current practice. To help reconsider feedback as a process for learning, this chapter first examines some common misconceptions about feedback then suggests a reconceptualization of a learning-focused feedback process. Finally, it defines the key concepts related to this approach.

Feedback misconceptions

There are many popular misconceptions about the content of feedback in the literature.

Most misconceptions about feedback result from a more traditional view of feedback as information transmitted to a learner by a knowledgeable other as a part of assessment or evaluation. Several relevant ones are discussed below.

Misconception 1: Feedback occurs only in performance evaluation.

The conception that has long existed in the "feedback avoidant" (Carroll, 2014) culture of many public and private organizations is that feedback occurs only during performance evaluation. This is understandable since most supervisors provide feedback during the dreaded annual performance review. When feedback is associated only with performance evaluation, it will continue to be sparse. In its *2013 State of the American Workplace Report,* Gallup reports that 70% of American workers are not fully engaged in their workplace. Of the 12 attributes Gallup uses to assess engagement, a factor consistently associated with high levels of organization performance, four directly relate to the presence of feedback. They are recognition or praise for doing good work in the past seven days; someone has talked to the employee about his progress; the presence of someone who encourages employee development; and opportunities at work to grow and learn within the past year (Gallup, 2013).

As the population of Millennials, who now make up a third of the workforce, grows as another third comprising Baby Boomers rapidly declines, the effect of employee engagement in the workplace is even more concerning, according to Gallup. In general, Millennials are less engaged at work than previous generations of workers. According to Gallup, "Millennials, who some have characterized as impatient to pay their dues, are most positive about growth and development opportunities at work" (p. 36). Millennials want frequent, honest feedback focused on their growth, unlike the feedback that generations of employees received in annual performance reviews. As the post-Millennials mature, exhibit more defined values and behaviors, and enter the workforce, they are likely to be resourceful, forthright, independent, and approach growth, learning, and engagement within organizations in yet different ways.

Misconception 2: People are feedback adverse.

Feedback is logical. Its absence in most organizations is illogical. Feedback as a process to promote growth is the fuel for improvement. When feedback is scarce, people lack knowledge to make changes in their practice. As a result, they may develop habits that are unproductive, inefficient, and difficult to change. When they have ongoing opportunity to understand expectations, have clear goals, know where they stand in relationship to

expectations, and clarify actions for changes, they are able to be more self-directed, continue to improve, feel more engaged, and feel better about their own performance.

Mark Murphy, CEO of Leadership IQ, conducted a study for LeadershipIQ. He concluded that employees want more opportunities to interact with their supervisors and when they do interact, their performance increases. He also reports that two-thirds of employees say they get too little positive feedback and over half say that they get too little constructive criticism. Yet, even when they receive positive or constructive criticism, those employees report that the feedback is insufficient to help them either repeat the practice or correct it (WorldatWork, 2009).

Misconception 3: The feedback sandwich softens critical feedback.

Some management advisors recommend the use of the feedback sandwich, critical feedback pressed between two slices of positive feedback. The ratio of two *glows* for every *grow* is a common practice. Raoul Buron and Dana McDonald-Mann (1999) recommend a ratio of 4:1, that is, four points of positive feedback for every one of negative feedback "creates the most favorable feedback climate" (p. 27). Others suggest that more positive feedback "shields the learner and teacher by balancing positive and negative feedback and thereby achieving personal preservation" (Kogan, et al., p. 212). They note that some medical faculty members use the positive to build a resident's confidence, receptivity, and trust. In reality, it may confuse learners or minimize the importance of the feedback. As Kogan and colleagues acknowledge, some faculty members report a strong sense of duty to be constructive in their feedback and develop the residents' comfort by engaging them in negative or critical feedback.

This misconception makes a fundamental assumption that an external partner is determining what is positive and negative, and that evaluating is a necessary part of the feedback process. While common as a component of performance evaluations or review, the feedback sandwich also has the potential to miscommunicate the intent, lessen the learner's motivation to act on the information, and eliminates the learner's opportunity to learn how to be analytic and independent.

Misconception 4: People prefer positive to negative feedback.

The direction of feedback, positive or negative, has been the subject of multiple studies over the years, yet results are inconclusive that one direction of feedback is preferable to or has a greater impact than the other. Learners usually understand that the purpose of the feedback process is to promote their growth. To that end, they want to be a part of a process that helps them understand how to improve. In the workplace this statement is more true for Millennials than for earlier generations of employees. In a study conducted among young technology and health care workers who were identified as top talent and high potential within their organizations, Anna Carroll (2014) reports that these employees believe that "negative or improvement feedback" (p. 14) is a way to facilitate their ongoing learning. They believe that if they had more feedback that was productive and constructive they would succeed faster. "Clearly when it comes to feedback," she adds, "younger workers want substance over style. The idea that a boss is softening or qualifying the delivery of a message seems foreign to them" (p. 15).

In their meta-analysis of feedback in K–12 education, Hattie and Timperley (2007) report that "studies showing the highest effect sizes involved [K–12] students receiving information feedback about a task and how to do it more effectively. Lower effect sizes were related to praise, rewards, or punishment" (p. 84).

In another meta-analysis of adult learner feedback interventions, Avraham Kluger and Angelo DeNisi (1996) found no difference in the direction of feedback, positive or negative, on its effects. In several subsequent experimental studies Kluger and DeNisi and others tested the effects of positive and negative feedback based on a hypothesis related to regulatory focus theory. Regulatory focus theory suggests two primary human drivers, promotion and prevention. Promotion-focused [adult] learners are interested in their growth and achievement of rewards. They view goals as desires and aspirations. Prevention-focused learners are more interested in responsibility and safety and are motivated by avoidance of pain and punishment. They view goals as necessities or obligations. When facing tasks that require creativity, people's motivation and performance increased with positive feedback. When facing tasks that required attention to detail and attention, people's motivation and performance decreased with positive feedback (Van Dijk & Kluger, 2011).

Common though they may be, these misconceptions contain the seeds of an approach to feedback as a process rather than a product. Misaligned practices can, with some care, practice, and guided effort, be adapted or adjusted so they more closely align with practices recommended throughout this book.

Reconceptualizing feedback for learning

Researchers in multiple arenas of education — K–12 education, higher education, and professional education — identify feedback as a significant factor in promoting effective teaching and learning practices. Yet, feedback is not so simple a process as it might seem. Christopher Watling, Erik Driessen, Cees van der Vleuten, and Lorelei Lingard (2014) point out that a 1996 meta-analysis demonstrated that feedback doesn't always have the effect intended. "It has become clear," they note, "that for feedback to be an effective facilitator of learning, it must be employed with great care" (p. 714).

This book is about how to employ care in thinking about and practicing the feedback process so that it results in learning.

John Hattie and Helen Timperley (2007) conclude that feedback for K–12 students is among the factors with strong effect size influencing learning and achievement, and Jack Ende's (1983) study of feedback in medical education reinforces the significance of feedback as a learning tool. It makes sense, then, to strengthen the use of feedback to promote the effectiveness of professional learning. Alex Bols and Kate Wicklow (2013) cite a common saying "within the National Union of Students [university students] (United Kingdom) that 'feedback is the breakfast of champions.' Just as breakfast is the most important meal of the day, so feedback is one of the most important elements for learning" (p. 19). They acknowledge that many students feel starved for lack of adequate feedback in higher education.

In Learning Forward's (2011) *Standards for Professional Learning,* feedback is associated with implementation of learning. Effective implementation includes constructive feedback as a part of the process for supporting the application of professional learning. With feedback, a learner is able to recognize how he integrates new learning, examine its impact on clients, and identify approaches to refining and strengthening practice to achieve high levels of effectiveness and results.

The Feedback Process: Transforming Feedback for Learning rests on two driving assumptions: The first is that learning is constructed through a process of engagement, analysis, and reflection and influenced by the context within which learning occurs and is applied. In his introduction to *Psychology of Learning,* William Mikulas defines learning as a "more or less permanent change in behavior potential that occurs as a result of practice," (p. xi). He notes that learning results from actual experience rather than from other influences such as "motivational factors, sensory adaptation, fatigue, maturation, senescence, or stimulus change" (p. xi). The second assumption is that the context within which learning occurs and is applied influences learning. In their chapter, "Cognition and Learning," James Greeno, Allan Collins, and Lauren Resnick (1996) describe three foundational perspectives that influence understanding of and research about learning. The perspectives are behaviorist, cognitivist, and situative, and together they influence educational practice. The authors advocate looking at the perspectives pluralistically to achieve the greatest value for understanding education.

These assumptions align with the constructivist and social interaction learning theories and Paulo Freire's (2006) principle of pedagogy. Both assumptions acknowledge that learning requires more than transmission of information. Rather, learning emerges from the process of constructing knowledge from authentic or simulated experience that immerses a learner in multisensory opportunities to apply and practice learning. This conceptualization of feedback creates new learning opportunities, which are defined more fully through the following terms.

Terms to know

Language influences how humans think and act. In this book, there will be rare references to feedback givers and receivers. These terms suggest that feedback is a product to be exchanged and that it is primarily unidirectional. In such a view of feedback, receivers are often passive recipients; moreover, givers and receivers hold different status.

To convey more clearly that feedback is a process rather than product, and that learning is the primary purpose of feedback, the terms *learner, learning partner, learning object, information,* and *knowledge* are used. The meaning of these terms is important for understanding the feedback process described in this book and realigning practices to support that process.

Learner is the person who actively engages in and even directs the feedback process. In the context of this book *learners* and *students,* unless specified, are both terms to mean "adults who are in post-secondary or professional learning situations." For most learners, the most common form of feedback is that which is received from another, yet internal feedback, for most learners, occurs continuously. Internal response, when acknowledged, becomes a powerful source of insight and motivation for future action. Learners may engage in the process independently using covert or overt processes. Covert processes include thinking about and reflecting *on* (considering after), *in* (considering during), and *for* (considering for future use) practice and the metacognitive processes associated with the practice. Some learners make their covert thinking external using overt processes such as journaling, discussing their thinking with a learning partner, or recording data about their practice. Whether internally

Terms for Understanding the Feedback Process

Learner is the person who actively engages in and even directs the feedback process.

Learning partner is someone who supports a learner in the feedback process.

Learning object is an artifact, experience, or pattern of behaviors that informs the feedback process and serves as evidence to analyze.

Information is simple and can be transmitted, recalled, and repeated without active engagement or higher levels of thinking.

Knowledge results from active construction of learning. Often associated with applying, analyzing, and evaluating situations to create new meaning or conclusions, generalizations, or theories for future action.

or externally generated through a process, the learner desires to refine, extend, alter, improve, or change understanding, skills, perspective, attitude, practice, and results.

Developing the capacity to engage in the feedback process, be self-analytical, reflect on practice, and refine practice are fundamental skills for all human beings. They are cultivated over time with opportunities to practice and with support from others within an environment conducive to learning, risk-taking, and experimenting. As learners mature and become more independent in the learning process, the significance of the independent application grows.

Learning partner is someone who supports a learner in the feedback process. A learning partner is a trusted peer or knowledgeable other.

Learning partners may be peers, supervisors, experts, consultants, mentors, coaches, students, or others with whom the learner interacts. Many would describe learning partners as givers of feedback. Supervisors, for example, provide regularly scheduled feedback as designated by a performance appraisal system. In this role, their goals may be twofold — to assess and evaluate as well as to support growth and improvement. Sometimes supervisors assume the role of a coach or consultant to provide formative feedback that may or may not be a component of a formal performance appraisal. Teachers, trainers, mentors, coaches, content experts, and consultants provide feedback, sometimes formally or informally as a part of their responsibilities and agreements with learners. Executive or performance coaches share feedback with their clients as a routine part of the coaching relationship. In an ideal relationship, the learning partner shapes the conversation to engage the learner in generating his or her own feedback. This approach to feedback serves three purposes: It leads to improved practice; it also helps the learner cultivate the expertise to self-analyze using explicit criteria and observable evidence. Lastly, it reinforces the value and habit of self-reflection.

Generally, learning partners have both a map for the feedback process and clarity about their roles in it, although there are cases in which partners may engage in the feedback process without a plan to do so. Sometimes, feedback occurs spontaneously so learners can take advantage of a learning opportunity. In other cases, feedback is intended to protect the safety or integrity of a learner or his clients. In such instances, unanticipated or unplanned feedback from a trusted learning partner is appropriate and may be welcome. Learners who are committed to continuous improvement are always open to opportunities that contribute to self-awareness, growth, and change in practice. When learning partners view feedback as occurring naturally within their organizations and a purposeful part of continuous professional growth, they become more observant, more open to learning, and better able to seek evidence in their routine practice and use it during the feedback process.

Learning object is an artifact, experience, or pattern of behaviors that initiates the feedback process and serves as evidence to analyze. A learning object might include an observed event, client- or learner-generated work samples, performance data, or a reflection on an experience.

Learning objects serve as evidence of learners' practices and stimuli for the learning process. The objects provide a source of information that learners analyze to construct knowledge and plan change. Having multiple forms of evidence from different sources provides different perspectives and enriches the analysis component of the feedback process. While the best forms of evidence are observable, tangible, and from multiple sources, intangible forms such as feelings are valid if made explicit through language. Examples of learning objects are described in the scenarios below.

A teacher may observe nonverbal behaviors among students that provide information with which the teacher makes a decision to alter course. While this feedback was not planned or sought, the teacher uses observed cues available within her environment as evidence within her continuous feedback process. Subsequently, she makes adjustments in her actions. Her observations of students' nonverbal cues serve as learning objects that informed her change.

An executive coach observes a leader facilitating the weekly management team meeting. During the visit to the team meeting, the coach is aware of the team members' silence, their sideways glances with each other, and their lack of eye contact with the leader. The coach is aware of these learning objects for the leader and the team. Stepping out of the silent observer role, he asks permission of the leader and team to make a public observation. They agree. His unplanned action initiates the feedback process in which the team and leader are able to construct together, through honest communication, knowledge about what is influencing the team's dynamics.

A mentor is co-teaching with a novice teacher. Their focus for the novice teacher is how to engage students in using evidence from the text. The novice teacher repeatedly accepts responses to her questions with no textual evidence. The mentor sees this pattern as a learning object. She steps next to the teacher and whispers a reminder about their shared

focus. The teacher responds by asking for evidence from the text in her next question.

A supervisor meets privately with a staff member to explore possible reasons and ways to address the staff member's repeated lateness to the leadership team meetings. The supervisor greets the staff member and shares the purpose of the meeting. The supervisor asks, "In what ways can I support you to arrive on time to the leadership team meetings?" Together the staff member and supervisor examine the competing commitments and priorities the staff member is juggling and how to prioritize them so that none interfere with the leadership team meeting.

In the examples above, the learning objects ranged from student nonverbal responses and client behaviors to learner behaviors. Each presents an opportunity for immediate or later learning through some form of feedback. The forms of feedback differ in the examples, yet the primary purpose remains the same — learning that strengthens practice.

Information is simple and can be transmitted, recalled, and repeated without active engagement or higher levels of thinking. Dates, facts, concept labels, principles, research findings, or theories can be recited with shallow or no understanding of their meaning or significance. Considered a low level of learning by Norman Webb (1999) and Benjamin Bloom (1956), information is a recall of facts, procedures, rules, guidelines, policies, skills that serve as the foundation for higher levels of learning. In Lorin Anderson et al. (2001), a revised approach to Bloom's Taxonomy, this lowest level is called *remembering*. By itself, this lowest level of learning — transmitted information that occurs most often from spoken or written sources — does not guarantee that the information is understood and acted upon, or integrated with other known information.

Knowledge, in this text, results from active construction of learning that occurs in complex thinking associated with applying, analyzing, and evaluating situations, experiences, information, data, or other learning objects to create new patterns, structuures, meaning, or conclusions, generalizations or theories for future action.

Building on John Seely Brown and Paul Duguid's work (2000) about information, Jan McArthur and Mark Huxham (2013) clarify the distinction between knowledge and information: "Knowledge is complex, contested and dynamic; there is a relationship between the knowledge and the knower and engagement with the knowledge is essential." They continue, "In contrast, information can be simpler; it can be passed over from one person to another with very little, if any active engagement" (p. 95). They go on to identify feedback not as simple information, but as knowledge

> with all of the attendant virtues and respect that deserves. If [adult] students are to be able to actively engage with feedback to be part of a dialogue, then that feedback cannot be presented, or regarded as a static canonical statement. By thinking of it in terms of knowledge to be discussed and interacted with by both parties [learner and learning partner(s)], we also introduce the notion that it is dynamic and

> contested: Not only do students have a right to challenge the feedback; they have a responsibility to determine for themselves its validity, usefulness and implication. (p. 95)

Knowledge is dynamic and situational; it is shaped by the context in which it exists, the learner, and others in the learning environment. It cannot be transmitted, only created and deconstructed. Knowledge is a product of reasoning about experiences and data. In the domains of learning described by both Anderson et al. (2001) and Webb (1999), knowledge occurs at the highest ends of the taxonomy or the deepest levels of cognitive learning. Constructing and deconstructing knowledge is the output of the feedback process that leads to more effective practice, and improved results are the outcomes of that feedback process.

Conclusion

Understanding the foundational concepts embedded in the feedback process described in this text will empower learners and learning partners to apply the feedback process to achieve transformation. Common misconceptions about feedback stem, most likely, from different notions about the purposes of feedback. Within the learning process, the role of feedback is clear. It is designed both to transform the learner and to cultivate learner expertise to engage in the highest form of feedback — self-generated, authentic, and unbiased feedback. With the ability to apply the feedback process at this level, a learner achieves self-determination and self-actualization that allows her to be deliberately critical in analysis and reflection of her own actions, words, and thoughts. Through honest, criteria-referenced assessment, a learner develops ability to identify strengths and gaps, set goals for continuous improvement, and map out a plan of action to achieve her learning goals.

At the end of each chapter, readers will be able to use reflection questions in reviewing major concepts and considering how to apply them to practice. In addition, readers may refer to the questions to make their own meaning of the main ideas based on their own experiences.

Reflections

1. This chapter presents several misconceptions about feedback. How do the misconceptions presented, and others you might add, begin to illuminate the critical aspects of learning-focused feedback?

2. How do the key terms differ from your current understanding of them? How might those differences affect your reading of this text?

3. Who are your formal and informal learning partners? How do you engage them in the feedback process?

4. The distinction between information and knowledge is fundamental to understanding the feedback process. Drawing on your own experience, describe that distinction and provide an example of each.

5. Consider a recent feedback experience you had. Which aspects aligned with the feedback process described in this chapter? Which aspects differed from the feedback process described in this chapter?

References

Anderson, L.W., Krathwohl, D.R., Airasian, P.W., Cruikshank, K.A., Mayer, R.E., Pintrich, P.R., Raths, J., & Wittrock, M.C. (2001). *A taxonomy for learning, teaching, and assessing: A revision of Bloom's Taxonomy of Educational Objectives.* New York, NY: Pearson and Allyn & Bacon.

Bloom, B. (1956). *Taxonomy of educational objectives: Cognitive and affective domains.* New York, NY: David McKay Company Inc.

Bols, A. & Wicklow, K. (2013). Feedback — what students want. In S. Merry, M. Price, D. Carless, & M. Taras (Eds.), *Reconceptualising feedback in higher education: Developing dialogue with students* (pp. 19–29). London, UK and New York, NY: Routledge.

Brown, J.S. & Duguid, P. (2000). *The social life of information.* Boston, MA: Harvard Business School Publishing Corporation.

Buron, R.J., & McDonald-Mann, D. (1999). *Giving feedback to subordinates.* Greensboro, NC: Center for Creative Leadership.

Ende, J. (1983). Feedback in clinical medical education. *JAMA,* 250(6), 777–78.

Freire, P. (2006). *Pedagogy of the oppressed, 30th anniversary edition.* New York, NY: Continuum.

Gallup, Inc. (2013). *The state of the American workplace: Employee engagement insights for U.S. business leaders.* Washington, DC: Author. Available at http://employeeengagement.com/wp-content/uploads/2013/06/Gallup-2013-State-of-the-American-Workplace-Report.pdf.

Greeno, J., Collins, A. & Resnick, L. (1996). Cognition and learning. In D. Berlinger & R. Calfee, (Eds). *Handbook of educational psychology,* (pp. 15–46). New York, NY: Macmillian.

Hattie, J. & Timperley, H. (2007). The power of feedback. *Review of Educational Research, 77*(1), 81–112.

Kluger, A. & DeNisi, A. (1996). The effects of feedback interventions on performance: historical review, a meta-analysis and a preliminary feedback intervention theory. *Psychological Bulletin, 119,* 254–284.

Learning Forward. (2011). *Standards for Professional Learning.* Oxford, OH: Author.

McArthur, J. & Huxham, M. (2013). Feedback unbound: From master to usher. In S. Merry, M., Price, D. Carless, & M. Taras (Eds.), *Reconceptualising feedback in higher education: Developing dialogue with students* (pp. 92–102). London, UK and New York, NY: Routledge.

Mikulas, W. (1977). Introduction: The nature of learning. In W. Mikulas (Ed.), *Psychology of learning: Readings* (pp. xi–xii). Chicago, IL: Nelson-Hall Publishers.

Van Dijk, D. & Kluger, A. N. (2011). Task type as a moderator of positive/negative feedback effects on motivation and performance: A regulatory focus perspective. *Journal of Organizational Behavior, 32*(8), 1084–1105. doi: 10.1002/job.725.

Watling, C., Driessen, E., van der Vleuten, C., & Lingard, L. (2014). Learning culture and feedback: An international study of medical athletes and musicians. *Medical Education, 48*(7), 713–723. Doi: 10.111/medu.1207.

Webb, N. L. (1999). *Alignment of science and mathematics standards and assessments in four states.* Madison, WI: National Institute for Science Education, University of Wisconsin-Madison.

WorldatWork. (2009, October 9). Employees want feedback, even if it's negative, study finds. Available at http://www.worldatwork.org/adimComment?id=34995.

Feedback Defined — and Redefined

IN THIS CHAPTER Readers review definitions of feedback from the research literature to expand the concept of feedback as static transmission of information to a dynamic, dialogic process of knowledge construction. Readers will:

- Study graphic depiction of the entire dialogic feedback process.
- Understand the sources and purposes of learning-focused feedback.
- Examine reflection questions about experiences with feedback.
- Use the tool to build a new definition of a learning-focused feedback process.

F eedback and the feedback process have multiple meanings. From education research literature alone, various definitions of feedback have emerged. This chapter outlines some of those definitions. and concludes with a definition that is used throughout this text and applies to the key attributes and fundamentals discussed in Chapter 3.

Feedback, in its early applications, was a process for controlling accuracy. From the efforts by Greeks and Arabs to use feedback controls to build clocks that kept accurate time to applications of mechanical signals made during the Industrial Revolution to maintain constancy, and finally to applications to create stability in automobile, aircraft, and spacecraft, feedback and feedback control systems are critical. They are the processes by which systems signal disturbances, disruptions, or errors and initiate actions to maintain a constant state. According to F.L. Lewis and Shuzhi Sam Ge (2006), *feedback control* involves computing suitable control inputs

> based on the difference between observed and desired behavior, for a dynamical system so the observed behavior coincides with a desired behavior prescribed by the user. All biological systems are based on feedback for survival, with even the simplest of cells using chemical diffusion based on feedback to create a potential difference across the membrane to maintain its *homeostasis,* or required equilibrium condition for survival. Volterra was the first to show that feedback is responsible for the balance of two populations of fish in a pond, and Darwin showed that feedback over extended time periods provides the subtle pressures that cause the evolution of species. (p. 791)

Likewise, as a part of the learning process, feedback generates disequilibrium and signals a need to act. This disequilibrium guides a learner to understand her current practice and initiates a stimulus to act. However, if the feedback process successfully informs the learning process, the action taken does not return the learner to a previous level of homeostasis, but moves her to a more refined level of practice closer to the ideal. In a sense feedback is, as Darwin described it, promoting evolution from the learner's current level of practice to a higher level of excellence. Whether generated internally by the learner or externally through engagement with a learning partner, the feedback process offers opportunities for change.

Definitions of Feedback

A common definition of feedback is a tool to close a gap in performance. More specifically, "feedback is information about the gap between the actual level and the reference level of a system parameter which is used to alter the gap in some way" (Ramaprasad, 1983, p. 4). In addition, there must be a clearly defined set of criteria to determine that a gap exists. D. Royce Sadler (1989) posits that feedback "requires knowledge of the standard or goal, skills in making multicriterion comparisons, and the development of ways and means for reducing the discrepancy between what is produced and what is aimed for" (p. 142).

John Hattie and Helen Timperley (2007), in their research synthesis on feedback in K–12 education, define feedback as "information provided by an agent (e.g. teacher, peer, book, parent, self, experience) regarding aspects of one's performance or understanding" (p. 81). The agent may be animate and inanimate. Feedback, they assert, is the "consequence of performance" (p. 81). Hattie and Timperley

emphasize that feedback cannot exist alone and be powerful. They stress the role of feedback as a part of the teaching-learning process. Feedback is a consequence of performance, and thus follows instruction. They stress that feedback is "part of the teaching process and is that which happens second — after a student has responded to initial instruction when information is provided regarding some aspect(s) of the student's task performance" (p. 82).

Deborah Butler and Phillip Winne (1994) drew from an extensive meta-analysis of studies on feedback to conclude that "feedback is information with which a learner can confirm, add to, overwrite, tune, or restructure information in memory, whether that information is domain knowledge, metacognitive knowledge, beliefs about self and tasks, or cognitive tactics and strategies" (p. 574).

Stephen Dinham (2008) defines feedback as

> any form of response by a teacher to a student's performance, attitude, or behaviour, at least where attitude or behaviour impinges upon performance. It is important to realise that feedback is not only an outcome of student performance but an essential part of the learning process. (p. 35)

David Boud and Elizabeth Molloy (2010) define feedback in higher and professional education as "a process whereby learners obtain information about their work in order to appreciate the similarities and differences between the appropriate standards for any given work, and the qualities of the work itself, in order to generate improved work" (p. 6).

Jennifer Kogan, Lisa Conforti, Elizabeth Bernabeo, Steven Durning, Karen Hauser, and Eric Holmboe (2012) define feedback in clinical practice as "specific information about the comparison between a trainee's observed performance and a standard given with the intent to improve the trainee's performance" (p. 202).

In their seminal work on feedback as a part of the assessment process, Paul Black and Dylan Wiliam (1998) state, "for the sake of simplicity, that the term feedback be used in its least restrictive sense, to refer to any information that is provided to the performer of any action about that performance" (p. 51). Black and Wiliam describe feedback as the product of assessment, and contend that there is not a need for an explicit set of criteria for a comparison, especially in the context of formative assessment.

According to Douglas Stone and Sheila Heen (2014), feedback is

> any information we get about ourselves. In the broadest sense, it is how we learn about ourselves from our experiences and from other people — how we learn from life… . Feedback is not just what gets ranked, it is what gets thanked, commented on, and invited back or dropped. Feedback can be formal or informal, direct or implicit; it can be blunt or baroque, totally obvious or so subtle that you're not sure what it is. (p. 4)

In *The Feedback Imperative*, Anna Carroll (2014) defines feedback as "information from past action that is used to guide future action" (p. 3). The feedback loop, she says, is the process of moving information from the past to the future.

As Maddalena Taras (2013) asserts, most discourse about feedback continues to include feedback as a one-way telling of information. She supports, as do her colleagues in the co-edited volume on feedback in higher education, *Reconceptualising Feedback in Higher*

Education: Developing Dialogue with Students (Merry, Price, Carless, & Taras, 2013), a view that feedback is a "dialogic, negotiated understanding" (p. 34) that results from the learner's voice and "within the domain and control of the learner" (p. 34).

Learning-focused feedback is based on the premise that the feedback process empowers and drives learners to learn rather than presumes that those who give feedback can cause them to learn (see Figure 2.1 on p. 14). This assumption requires redefining feedback as it is traditionally understood and presented in some literature. This new definition, then, is based on an analysis of the literature and reconceptualizes it for use within the arena of professional learning and growth.

For the purposes of this book, feedback is defined as a dynamic, dialogic process that uses evidence to engage a learner, internally or with a learning partner, in constructing knowledge about practice and self. Figure 2.1: The Feedback Process on page 14 shows that the process begins with a learner and a learning object, which is an experience or a pattern of behaviors, for example, an instructional practice such as facilitating student discussion of complex texts. The feedback process proceeds through analysis of data and evidence to build the learner's capacity to engage in social interaction, metacognition, self-analysis, and reflection. As a result, the learner may construct new knowledge about her practice and, later, deconstruct that knowledge to examine variations, alternatives, or applications in other meanings and contexts. An effective feedback process helps a learner generate a deep understanding of current practice — how the practice affects and is affected by the learner, her clients, and environment; and how it relates to established criteria of excellence. In a cycle, the feedback process guides the learner in planning and taking future actions to move practice closer to the desired level.

This proposed definition extends the concept of feedback well beyond static information. It emphasizes the dynamic and dialogic process of construction rather than transmission of information. It results in a learner not only in knowing his or her current state, but also what to do to move toward a more desirable level. By engaging in the feedback process a learner builds independence with rigorous, objective, and deep self-generated analysis as well as constructs new knowledge about one's practice and oneself. In its highest form, the feedback process leads the learner through

Figure 2.1: **The Feedback Process**

deconstruction of the new knowledge to examine variations in meaning and situational applications of the newly constructed knowledge.

To fully understand the learning-focused feedback process, it is essential to examine some key aspects of the proposed definition: the source and purpose of the feedback process.

Source of the feedback process

There are three basic sources of the feedback process — unidirectional, conversational, and self-generated. Each is appropriate for some situations, yet none functions equally well in all situations. Identifying the direction of the feedback process describes who drives the process. The feedback directions and their sources are described below.

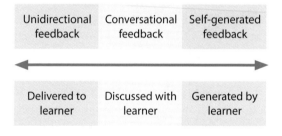

Unidirectional feedback. Unidirectional feedback is information generated by someone external to the learner. It is transmitted to the learner as a product rather than as a process. In other words, a teacher, coach, supervisor, peer, mentor, or knowledgeable other shares feedback with the learner. While these largely unidirectional conversations may include some discussion about the learner's understanding of the feedback or proposed actions for improvement, they are typically one-sided conversations in which there is both a clearly defined giver and receiver of the information. Unidirectional feedback frequently occurs as a part of performance appraisal in which a supervisor evaluates performance, shares the evaluation, and sets goals for future performance. Unidirectional feedback processes are also common when there are risks to the learner or others. When a learner practicing how to use a new piece of equipment needs a correction to prevent damage to herself or the equipment, swift unidirectional feedback is appropriate. When teachers are learning to make the appropriate instructional shifts related to implementing mathematical practices, they may be told to decrease the amount of specific direction they give students and encourage students to engage in more productive struggle. Supervisors learning to employ new observation tools when they visit teachers' classrooms might be directed to record what students are doing in addition to what teachers are doing to increase the accuracy of their observation.

Conversational feedback. As feedback moves away from the unidirectional to a shared process, the learner engages in a conversation with an external learning partner about his practice and his understanding of its relationship to ideal practice. A learner may be invited to share his reflections on the learning object, response to a learning partner's perceptions or data collected, or share ideas about next actions. Yet, even though a learner is more engaged, he does not share full ownership of the feedback process. The learning process is facilitated and usually driven by a learning partner who has predetermined a major portion of the conversation's outcome, often based on data or evidence drawn from one or more learning objects. For example, a learning partner may determine in advance that the learner needs to focus attention on communicating more directly with peers. To engage the learner in conversation about communication, the learning partner has a predetermined plan for the sequence of the conversation, intended outcome of the conversation, and specific practices to recommend.

This fairly common approach to feedback is used by learning partners who are more knowledgeable others and who are often responsible for assessing or judging a learner's practice. These conversations are common between mentors and novices, coaches and their clients, supervisors and supervisees, or among peers. In such conversations, learners and their learning partners collaboratively analyze data, generate learning from their analysis, and plan next actions. As the work of the learning partner becomes more refined, she may be less likely to feel compelled to lead the learner toward her ideas and may use the conversational approach to move closer to a self-generated feedback process.

Self-generated feedback. The self-generated feedback process, a refined form of cognitive behavior, occurs with or without a learning partner. It is generated by the learner and includes authentic, honest, and objective self-analysis that promotes metacognition, reflection, construction of new knowledge, and deconstruction of that knowledge to question its meaning and application in diverse situations. A learner who achieves this capacity engages in this process with deliberate intention free from self-deception. Psychologists from Abraham Maslow, Erik Erikson, to Carl Rogers and others identify the capacity of individuals to achieve their potential, resolve dichotomies, and find meaning in life as the highest level of achievement in human existence. Richard Paul (2012) labels this level of thinking as critical thinking in the *strong* sense.

In a self-generated feedback process, the learning partner, when present, serves as a facilitator and listening partner who clarifies,

probes, and summarizes the learner's cognitive processes, yet remains neutral about the learner's knowledge. The learning partner is a process facilitator, not a content expert. In fact, learning partners with strong experience or deep knowledge about the practice a learner is refining may find it difficult to remain content neutral, often because they have formed their own perception of effective and ineffective practice and want to be helpful. Help, when given in the feedback process as information, diminishes the learner's examination of his or her own practice and thus violates the fundamental assumption that learning emerges from practice.

Self-generated feedback is neither required nor appropriate in all situations. While the ultimate goal is to cultivate an individual's capacity for self-generated feedback, in some feedback situations unidirectional or conversational feedback may be more appropriate. When learners are unable to be objective about their own practice, may benefit from the expertise of a knowledgeable other to achieve advanced levels of learning, or want to validate their own self-analysis with an external learning partner, they may turn to another for either unidirectional or conversational feedback. Kogan, et al. (2012) state that because self-assessment is often inadequate, external feedback helps learners understand "what they are doing well and what requires improvement" (p. 202).

Purpose of the feedback process

Feedback serves multiple purposes. Douglas Stone and Sheila Heen (2014) acknowledge that feedback has the potential to meet multiple purposes. "In today's workplace, feedback plays a crucial role in developing talent, improving morale, aligning teams, solving problems, and boosting the bottom line" (p. 5). The feedback process, whether internally or externally generated, results in the construction of knowledge that leads to change in perception, attitude, knowledge, skill, and practice. This premise is fundamental throughout this book.

The feedback process then may be designed to lead educators to replace practices that are ineffective; refine practice so that it more closely aligns with criteria of excellence; raise consciousness about how their current practice aligns with specified criteria; and generate self-awareness and the ability to self-evaluate performance. Feedback process contributes to building a collaborative, learning-focused culture, especially when peers engage in the feedback process with each other and share the knowledge constructed from the process. Most often, feedback serves learning-focused or growth-oriented purposes, including increasing one's level of performance by refining or revising strategies, increasing one's commitment and motivation to learn and grow, expanding understanding of one's experiences and their implications for future experiences, and re-working, refining, and reordering knowledge, attitudes, skills, and practices. Its primary purpose, one that is a core premise of this book, is learning that guides change.

Partners agree on purpose. During the feedback process, the learner and learning partner mutually agree on a purpose for the feedback process before they begin. In cases in which a learner is unable to determine or influence the purpose, he should, at least, be aware of the purpose in advance. For example, in an authentic practice situation in which a learner's practice has the potential to risk the safety or well-being of another, a learning partner might announce in advance that he will interrupt practice if there is imminent danger. Having

a clear and stated purpose for the feedback process whether internal or externally driven gives focus and clarity to the process and may minimize perceived discomfort or anxiety.

Factors affect achievement of purpose. Several factors influence whether the feedback process approaches or achieves its purpose. The most important condition that affects the outcome of the feedback process is the learner. How the learner interprets the feedback, the meaning she makes of it, the relationship she has with the source of feedback and the learning partner, the environment within which the feedback process occurs, and the learner's emotional state all influence how well feedback promotes learning. The resulting change and the learner's deep awareness of how his actions influence himself, others, and the environment are ultimate measures of the effectiveness of the feedback process. Not all feedback achieves its desired purpose. Some learners might disregard, dispute, or dismiss the feedback process. Sometimes the feedback process initiates actions that are misaligned with the desired practice. At other times, the feedback process might challenge a learner's self-confidence or esteem and reduce his motivation to change. Clarity of purpose of the feedback process, both on the part of the learner and learning partner, can mitigate these unproductive effects.

When feedback is treated as a product transmitted by an external source to another, there is the possibility that the receiver may question the trustworthiness of the source and veracity of the feedback. Lack of trust may especially be the case when receiver does not perceive the external source to be a learning partner engaged in the feedback process. When feedback is a shared responsibility among the learner, learning partner(s), and the environment, feedback is more likely to be trusted, particularly when there is congruence among them and clear criteria for performance. Even for learners who have refined the self-generated feedback process, the environment and cultural norms may be factors in promoting or restricting the process. When it is a normative process among professionals who share collective responsibility for each other's success and that of their clients, feedback encourages continuous improvement. It supports examination of practice and results in a routine process and cultivates the desire to achieve high levels of performance and outcomes.

At the end of this chapter, Tool 2.1: *Building a new definition of the feedback process* lets readers consider their perspectives on the components of the feedback process focused on learning.

Conclusion

Feedback alone, regardless of its source or purpose, is insufficient to support efficient and effective growth and change in behavior. It is the feedback process that leads to achieving results, especially when the feedback process is designed to develop knowledge, skills, and practices and motivation to act upon the feedback to generate results. When the feedback process is integrated into a comprehensive system of learning and continuous improvement, incorporates learning goals, focuses on future actions, and occurs within a safe environment with necessary supports, it is more likely to result in productive change in practice and cultivate refined ability for self-analysis within learners.

Reflections

1. The chapter offers various definitions of feedback. Of those offered, which is most closely aligned to the definition you held about feedback before you read this chapter? Explain.

2. What assumptions do you hold about the feedback process? The definition the author proposes is based on a set of assumptions. Which assumptions align with those you hold and which are ones differ from your own assumptions?

3. How do the sources and purposes of feedback described in this chapter align with your current experiences and practices with feedback?

4. Describe several situations in which you would use unidirectional feedback, conversational feedback, and self-generated feedback. What factors influenced your choice of each type? Under what circumstances might each source of feedback be appropriate in the same situation?

5. What factors or circumstances might prompt you to dismiss, disregard, or dispute feedback? What factors might cause you to question the integrity and trustworthiness of a learning partner? Consider how understanding these factors might influence your feedback practice.

References

Black, P. & Wiliam, D. (1998). Assessment and classroom learning. *Assessment in Education, 5*(1), 7–74.

Butler, D. L. & Winne, P.H. (1995). Feedback and self-regulated learning: A theoretical synthesis. *Review of Educational Research, 65*(3), 245–281.

Carroll, A. (2014). *The feedback imperative: How to give everyday feedback to speed up your team's success.* Austin, TX: River Grove Books.

Dinham, S. (2008). Powerful teacher feedback. *Synergy, 4*(2), 35–38.

Erikson, E. (1980). *Identity and the life cycle.* New York, NY: W.W. Norton and Company.

Hattie, J. & Timperley, H. (2007). The power of feedback. *Review of Educational Research, 77*(1), 81–112.

Kogan, J., Conforti, L., Bernabeo, E., Durning, S., Hauser, K., & Holmboe, E. (2012). Faculty perceptions of feedback to residents after direct observation of clinical skills. *Medical Education, 46*(2), 201–215.

Lewis, F.L. & Ge, S.S. (2006). Neural networks in feedback control systems. In M. Kutz (Ed.), *Mechanical engineers' handbook, Volume 2: Instrumentation, systems, controls, and MEMS, 3rd edition* (pp. 791–825). New York, NY. doi: 10.1002/0471777455.

Maslow, A. (1988). *Toward a psychology of being, 3rd edition.* New York, NY: John Wiley and Sons.

Paul, R.W. (2012). *Critical thinking: What every person needs to survive in a rapidly changing world.* Tomales, CA: Foundation for Critical Thinking.

Ramaprasad, A. (1983). On the definition of feedback. *Behavioral Sciences, 28*(1), 4–13.

Rogers, C. (1961). *On becoming a person: A distinguished therapist's view on personal growth and creativity.* New York, NY: Houghton Mifflin Company.

Sadler, D.R. (1989). Formative assessment in the design of instructional systems. *Instructional Science, 18*(2), 119–144.

Stone, D. & Heen, S. (2014). *Thanks for the feedback: The science and art of receiving feedback well.* New York, NY: Viking.

Taras, M. (2013). Feedback on feedback: Uncrossing wires across sectors. In S. Merry, M. Price, D. Carless, & M. Taras (Eds.), *Reconceptualising feedback in higher education: Developing dialogue with students* (pp. 30–40). London, UK and New York, NY: Routledge.

TOOL 2.1

Building a new definition of the feedback process

Use this tool to reflect on the reconceptualized definition of the feedback process. The left-hand column includes the key components of the definition of learning-focused feedback. Consider your perspective about each and jot your thoughts in the right-hand column. Add any components of the definition you think might be missing and explain their importance.

Definition components	Reflections on definition
Dynamic, dialogic process	
Uses evidence to engage the learner in constructing knowledge about practice and self	
Occurs internally or externally	
Generates deep understanding of • Current practice; • How practice affects and is influenced by the learner, the learner's clients, and the environment; • How it relates to established criteria of excellence	
Guides the learner to plan and take future actions to move practice closer to desired level	
Builds the learner's capacity to engage in metacognition, self-analysis, and reflection	
Constructs new knowledge about the learner's practice and contexts	

Attributes of an Effective Feedback Process

IN THIS CHAPTER

Readers learn about 11 attributes of an effective feedback process focused on learning. Readers will:

- Compare and contrast attributes of traditional feedback with learning-focused feedback process.
- Examine reflection questions about experiences with feedback.
- Use tools to test their readiness to undertake a learning-focused feedback process.

Not all feedback is created equal. Actually, it is quite uneven in its design and effectiveness. Feedback forms typically used by educators and the feedback process used to support learning have markedly different attributes. Understanding the key attributes of effective feedback is important for those involved in the feedback process. This chapter contrasts attributes of traditional feedback with those of the learning-focused feedback process as identified from the literature review for this book.

The most typical forms of feedback are those that occur in a conversation between or among people. With a learner committed to continuous improvement, the feedback process occurs frequently, almost constantly, internally in the form of self-initiated reflection and analysis. Whether the feedback process is externally or internally driven, the same attributes apply. The attributes of an effective feedback process are based on the premise that the

feedback process generates learning that leads to change in practice. The process increases a learner's consciousness about her practice and the impact of those practices on others and the environment in which they occur. By increasing awareness of the interactions among her own actions, those of others, and the environment, a learner gains the ability to assess whether her actions were effective, to consider alternative actions, and to plan for and refine future actions.

Table 3.1 on page 22 displays how learning-focused feedback differs from some forms of traditional feedback. Examining the contrast in attributes might influence learners and learning partners as they shift their feedback practice toward learning-focused feedback.

Thus, attributes of learning-focused feedback serve as guidelines for both the learner who engages in self-generated feedback process and for those who serve as learning partners. Clearly, not all feedback

Table 3.1: **Contrasts Between Traditional and Learning-focused Feedback**

Traditional feedback	Learning-focused feedback
Product	Process
Opinion/judgment	Criteria-based
Single form/source of data/evidence	Multiple forms and sources of data/evidence
Expected	Desired
Untimely	Timely
Impersonal	Responsive to learner
Occasional	Frequent
Past-focused	Future-focused
One-way	Reciprocal
Communicated	Skillful interaction
One dimension	Multidimensional

meets all criteria. The following attributes provide guidelines for shaping the feedback process so that it has the greatest potential to produce learning and subsequent change in practice.

Effective feedback is a process. Feedback is a process that engages a learner in review, analysis, reflection, and planning of future action. Too often feedback is considered a product — information that includes some critique or assessment of performance with specific guidance or direction for corrective action or improvement. When viewed as a product, feedback typically needs a giver, someone who crafts the information and shares it with the receiver. Feedback in this form may have less potential to generate willingness for future refinements or improvements and may do little to cultivate a level of self-analysis and reflection that are the hallmarks of a learned person. When learners actively engage in constructing feedback rather than in passively receiving feedback, they are far more likely to own the information generated and to take responsibility for future actions.

Effective feedback process is criteria-based. The feedback process uses explicit, pre-established, and known criteria or expectations as a referent for analysis and construction of knowledge. Explicit criteria define expectations against which practice is assessed and next actions generated. The criteria for success may be defined in performance standards, rubrics, criteria lists, checklists, innovation configuration maps, or other forms. Without explicit criteria known to the learner and the learning partner, it is difficult to determine where a learner's current practice is in relationship to the expected or desired performances. It is essential to the learning process that a learner knows what the expected or desired goals are and what constitutes excellent practice. Without this knowledge, learners are challenged to plan next actions to advance practice to higher levels. When criteria are absent or unknown, the feedback process may be or be perceived to be judgmental or biased. Clear criteria increase the objectivity, focus, and purpose in the feedback process and help the learner choose appropriate tactics to move closer to the desired or expected levels of performance.

Effective feedback process integrates multiple forms of data converted into evidence. Multiple forms and sources of data transformed into evidence are more instructive, concrete, less biased, and subjective. They also facilitate and expand a learner's understanding and contribute to the construction of knowledge. Evidence increases the veracity of the feedback process. Using evidence about specific practices and their impact contributes to a learner's perceived value of the feedback. Valuing the feedback, in turn, increases the learner's motivation to use the knowledge constructed to adjust. Evidence may include data collected from direct observations of practice, analysis of work products, input from clients the learner interacts with, such as students providing their perceptions of their learning experiences to help a teacher analyze the impact of his practice, of a learner's reflection on practice prompted by a protocol or questions to guide analysis and metacognition.

Effective feedback process is desired. When the feedback process is invited and welcome, it is a gift; when unwelcomed and uninvited, it may generate defensiveness. The feedback process has greater meaning and value to a learner who believes that he is capable of and committed to continuous improvement and who is surrounded by needed supports. When the learner has a learning partner, the process is enhanced when both partners want to learn and refine their practice and when both partners hold a belief in their own potential to grow and learn. The learner especially must acknowledge that she is responsible for her own success and, as a result, have a strong sense of efficacy and agency.

Learning new practices requires that learners engage in four actions: (a) apply the learning in authentic contexts, (b) refine the practices

over time, (c) keep a goal-driven fidelity to criteria of excellence, and (d) assess the results of the practices. When they do these things, learners are better able to construct knowledge based on the feedback process and use it guide them in adjusting how they apply the lessons. A learner's receptivity to and use of feedback increases when she is willing to improve, is open to feedback, and has a desire to learn so she can achieve identified goals and meet expected criteria. When learners believe that they do not need to change, they are less likely to want feedback; thus, they resist constructing new knowledge that might differ from their existing knowledge. When learners have no desire to improve, they make no effort to alter future actions. Cultivating a desire for learning from the feedback process is an essential attribute of the feedback process.

Effective feedback process is timely. The proximity of the feedback process to specific practice influences how the learner responds to the opportunity to learn. If the feedback process occurs immediately, the learner is able to remember details of the specific experience. If the feedback process happens days later, the learner may not remember important details of the practice; therefore, he may lose some capacity to understand, engage in, or value the feedback process. With a long timespan between practice and feedback, the learner is likely to receive reinforcement to continue a practice that actually needs alteration. Conversely, a longer timespan may benefit a learning situation in which learners routinely and effectively engage in a self-generated feedback process. A learner may appreciate having some time to undertake his own self-analysis before engaging with an external learning partner. Afterward, the results of the self-generated feedback process can be artfully integrated into the external feedback process. By scaffolding internal feedback with prompts in the form of questions or areas to explore, an external learning partner focuses the internal feedback process and prepares the learner to be more actively engaged with her in analysis, reflection, and future planning. Time, in such a case, may reinforce the value of self-analysis and reflection.

Effective feedback process is responsive to the learner. Feedback is more likely to be valued and understood when the feedback process is tailored to the developmental needs and learning preferences of the learner, the learner's level of expertise, and the context in which the practice occurs. Some learners want more direct feedback while others may want to generate their own feedback. Learners have different dominant intelligences or cognitive information processing styles that affect how they perceive an experience, engage within the feedback process, construct knowledge, and use it in future action. For example, learners with strong visual intelligence might find graphs, charts, diagrams, or other learning tools helpful to facilitate the engagement in the feedback process. Learners for whom the process is new may benefit from more detailed, specific guidance. Learners for whom the learning is familiar and who are practicing it might benefit from exploring other domains of learning such as their affective or emotional intelligence. The feedback process can prompt metacognition, thinking about their decision making, cognitive processes, emotional triggers, and behavioral choices. Examining feelings associated with particular experiences might provide insights into choices made such as when a teacher becomes frustrated with students' behaviors and responds to students inappropriately.

Effective feedback process is frequent. A climate of trust, risk-taking, collaborative support, transparency, and continuous improvement encourages frequent feedback. For that reason frequent and routine feedback processes tend to be viewed as growth-oriented. In a climate of fault finding, competition, and privatization, the feedback process increases defensiveness and reduces the opportunity for it to generate learning. When the feedback process is rare, occasionally scheduled, or only associated with performance evaluation processes, it may be interpreted as evaluation, chastisement, reprimand, or censure. This is the typical response when the feedback process occurs only within formal situations such as personnel appraisal systems. Such an episodic approach to feedback process makes it a high-stakes event, and as a result may influence how learners respond to feedback. Unless the learner values and perceives that this form of feedback is designed to promote growth, appraisal, or evaluation feedback may be received simply as a perfunctory part of employment. When the feedback process is routine and includes engagement with multiple external learning partners and internally generated processes, learners are more likely to be open to and use the feedback process to make continuous adjustments in their practices.

Effective feedback process is future-focused. Feedback that guides the learner toward changes in subsequent practice helps a learner move toward the defined goal in an expedient way. Future-focused rather than past-focused feedback promotes next-action thinking and use of the feedback. Feedback that weaves in opportunities for planning for future action supports the integration of the feedback to alter practice. Feedback that rehashes the past without intentionally addressing potential changes may leave the learner unsure about what next actions to take or how to alter practice to achieve the desired goal.

Effective feedback process is reciprocal. The feedback process includes reciprocity. That is, learning partners help each other grow. Through the feedback process, a learner helps her learning partner construct knowledge to build the partner's capacity to contribute productively to the process. The learning partner, with help from the learner, reflects on the feedback conversation to analyze it and strengthen how she facilitates and structures future feedback conversations. In internal feedback processes, a learner analyzes and reflects on her metacognition, application of critical thinking, and future actions. For feedback to become routine within an organization, it must flow across hierarchical levels, be woven into a variety of different interactions, occur with gracious appreciation for the opportunity to learn, and focus on refining how people engage, either together or alone, in the feedback process. They routinely provide opportunities for the feedback process within informal as well as formal interactions. Learning partners model their commitment to the feedback process as a vehicle for continuous improvement by asking learners to become their partners as they construct new knowledge about their roles. For example, after Justin serves as a learning partner for Muriel, he asks her to act as his learning partner and help him examine his practice as a learning partner.

Internal and external feedback processes require deliberate thought, time for deep analysis and reflection, opportunities to plan and practice refinements, and commitment to continual learning. The process deserves priority in importance and time. Visible evidence that supervisors and informal leaders value the feedback process to construct knowledge leads to improved practice and increased results. Indicators that leaders value the feedback process include setting aside time for the feedback process, inviting others to serve as their learning partners, sharing the knowledge they constructed from the feedback process, and identifying and reflecting on behavior changes they are making. Using the key attributes of the feedback process as guidelines may facilitate more effective engagement in the feedback process. They serve as a reminder about what distinguishes learning-focused feedback from other forms of feedback and may help learning partners and learners increase their competency with the process.

Effective feedback process employs skillful interaction. The feedback process requires clarity. When self-generated, the learner uses clear, precise language to make her thinking explicit. Journaling, self-dialogue, or self-talk are possible ways to making thinking explicit or overt. Engaging in conversation with a learning partner requires both a learner and her learning partner to be precise in their communication with each other to increase understanding. If a learner is unclear about terms used, misinterprets the nuances of tone, pitch, nonverbals, or volume, or processes information differently than the learning partner, the meaning-making process is confounded. Skillful communication is essential for accuracy and understanding. In many cases the value of feedback process depends on how it is understood and used to shape future actions. External feedback processes occur in conversations that rely on listening fully, paraphrasing, and summarizing; using precise, unbiased, jargon-free, and action-oriented language; pausing; asking powerful questions that prompt deep thinking, analysis, reflection, and construction of new knowledge. Such conversations occur best when both the learner and learning partner are committed to honesty, integrity, and a shared purpose.

Effective feedback process is multidimensional. Multidimensional feedback engages the learner in more than one way. It helps the learner reflect in multiple ways that tap various types of learning. Some forms of learning may be more influential in helping a learner strengthen her practice. The cognitive level focuses on what the learner knows. The behavioral level examines what a learner does. The metacognitive level explores how the learner processes information, makes decisions, and makes sense of his or her experience. The emotional level engages the learner at the feeling level. The belief level engages the learner in identifying his underlying beliefs and assumptions that prompt actions, words, and thoughts. The aspirational level engages a learner in examining motivation or drivers. Learners who examine practice from multiple dimensions and levels gain a deeper understanding of their practice from the feedback process. Multidimensional feedback opens channels for analysis that might remain closed

and takes advantage of expanded opportunities to promote learning for refined practice.

Two tools in this chapter support learners and learning partners in applying the key attributes of the feedback process into their routine work. Tool 3.1: *Feedback process readiness* and Tool 3.2: *Post-feedback process assessment* are designed to help learners and learning partners determine their readiness for the feedback process and their engagement in it.

Conclusion

Feedback is not the same as the feedback process. And not all feedback leads to learning and change. Knowing the attributes of the feedback process helps the practitioner understand whether she is giving feedback to someone who will receive it or engaging a learner in a feedback process as a partner in the learning. When the purpose of feedback is judgment rather than learning, the many attributes of the effective feedback process are often missing. This distinction is an important consideration for those who use feedback as a tool for change.

Reflections

1. The feedback process has multiple attributes. How do the attributes identified vary in significance? In other words, which attributes do you consider more significant or essential than others? Explain your thinking.

2. What other attributes of the effective feedback process are not included here?

3. Considering your own feedback practice, which attributes are strengths for you? What might be possible contributing factors to these particular attributes being strengths?

4. Considering the norms related to feedback in your organization, which attributes are less common? What might be potential contributing factors to this normative situation?

5. Which of the attributes are ones you want to intentionally integrate into your practice? What are some tactics for attending to these attributes?

Feedback process readiness

As you prepare for the feedback process, ask yourself, "How am I addressing each key attribute?" In the second column below, jot a note about how you plan to address each attribute to assess your readiness to enter the feedback process. For example, in response to "is criteria-based," you might note that you will have the performance standards and rubric available for reference.

Key attributes of effective feedback	How am I addressing this attribute?
Is a process	
Is criteria-based	
Integrates multiple forms and sources of data/evidence	
Is desired	
Is timely	
Is responsive to learner	
Is frequent	
Is future-focused	
Is reciprocal	
Employs skillful interaction	
Is multidimensional	

Post-feedback process assessment

As you reflect on the feedback process you participated in, ask yourself, "How did I attend to each attribute and what might I want to do to strength how I integrate each into the feedback process?" In the second and third columns, record your responses. For example, in response to "is a process," you might rate your inclusion of this attribute a 2. In the third column, you might note that you want to shift from giving information to facilitating the construction of knowledge by talking less, listening more, and asking powerful questions.

Key attributes of effective feedback	How well did I attend to this attribute? On a scale of 1 (not well) – 3 (well)?	What do I want to do to strengthen my feedback process?
Is a process		
Is criteria-based		
Integrates multiple forms and sources of data/evidence		
Is desired		
Is timely		
Is responsive to learner		
Is frequent		
Is future-focused		
Is reciprocal		
Employs skillful interaction		
Is multidimensional		

Feedback Conditions

Readers examine the conditions needed to engage a learner with the components of an effective feedback process focused on learning: learner's mindset, learning environment, learning partners, and learning tasks. Readers will:

- Delve deeply into understanding how to prepare learners and learning partners to share and accept feedback to advance learning.

- Reflect on questions about the conditions needed for learning-focused feedback and how to develop conditions in their schools and districts.

- Use the tools to analyze the conditions for a learning-focused feedback process and the critical thinking that supports the cognitive conditions.

For the feedback process to achieve its intended result of change in practice, it is important to create the conditions that will engage the learner in constructing and deconstructing knowledge, taking action on that knowledge, and becoming more independent in the process as he does so. The process requires an unmasking of deep-seated assumptions and routines that may be initially uncomfortable for the learner, especially one who has experienced more traditional approaches to feedback. This chapter examines the conditions that create a safe place for transparency, deep analysis, and ruthless honesty.

The conditions in which the feedback process takes place influence the outcome. Harold Bok, Pim Teunissen, Annemarie Spruijt, Joanne Fokkemam, Peter von Beukelen, Debbie Jaarsma, and Cees van der Vleuten (2013), conclude that the learning climate along with the learning partner's capacity for facilitating the feedback process "promotes or deters [adult]

students' feedback-seeking behavior" (p. 290). They advise that it is essential to "create an environment that facilitates the use of active feedback-seeking strategies" (p. 290).

For the feedback process to be effective in promoting change, *conditions in which it occurs must be conducive to learning*. Those conditions include three distinct interrelated elements. The first is the learner's mindset, including her readiness for learning. The second is the learning environment in which feedback occurs. This includes relationships between the learner and others, the culture in which learning occurs, and trust among learning partners. The third is the nature of the learning task. This chapter explores these crucial conditions for feedback.

Learner's mindset

The mental framework of the learner plays a substantive role in the feedback process. The learner's mindset, whether fixed or growth-oriented, as Carol Dweck confirms, is instrumental in determining how people's beliefs shape their potential and influence their behavior and success. "This growth mindset is based on the belief that your basic qualities are things that you can cultivate through your efforts. Though people may differ in every which way — their initial talents, aptitudes, interests, or temperaments — everyone can grow and change through application and experience" (p. 7). A growth mindset stimulates effort and willingness within a learner to move feedback from information to knowledge and to use it to shape future action. Learners thrive on challenges and use failure as an opportunity for growth and learning; they seek information that helps them refine existing practice. Engagement in the feedback process not only generates new knowledge, but it also builds motivation to carry out the action. Such levels of persistence and agency lead to additional feedback that increases learners' effectiveness and results.

A fixed mindset, on the other hand, is based on the assumption that traits, abilities, even intelligence, are static and that little change will occur in them. Success is an affirmation of the abilities a person possesses. A desire to avoid failure, prove success, and seek approval or validation drives those with fixed mindsets. Learners with fixed mindsets fear feedback because it may illuminate inadequacies they are unwilling to acknowledge. This fear leads learners to tune out feedback about how to improve. When a learner believes he has achieved a level of excellence with a practice, he is unlikely to want to improve.

Dweck's research confirms that the orientation of fixed and growth mindsets occur very early in life. Yet, if learners and learning partners persist in cultivating a growth

mindset through their interactions with each other, even those with fixed mindsets can be moved. Frequent engagement in the feedback process, encouragement for self-generated feedback, serving as a learning partner for others, support for learning, and acknowledging effort are some ways to adapt mindsets toward a growth orientation.

Readiness for feedback

Readiness for feedback involves preparing oneself for learning. Readiness combines skillfulness to engage in the feedback process, mindfulness to be able to perceive the world in different ways, and openness to new discoveries. Douglas Stone and Sheila Heen (2014) note, feedback is about "your willingness to show that you don't have it all figured out, and to bring your whole self — flaws, uncertainties, and all — into the relationship" (p. 290).

Readiness is an emotional, physical, and cognitive state. As an emotional state, it involves one's identify, confidence, and esteem. When learners are healthy, rested, nourished, and comfortable, they are better equipped physically for learning. Cognitively, feedback requires the application of creative and critical thinking and reasoning skills.

Emotional state. When learners are emotionally neutral, feel comfortable with others involved in the feedback process, and perceive no danger, they are ready for feedback. If learners understand in advance that the feedback process may result in unexpected discoveries that illuminate differences between self-perceived strengths or growth areas and another's perception of them, learners may be unable to prevent their brain's limbic system and its core component the amygdala from leaping into avoidance or defensive behaviors to protect one's identity or self-concept.

Such responses trigger the fight or flight mechanism within the brain. Fighting responses may include challenging the validity of the data, blaming others for the circumstances, or questioning the competence or integrity of learning partners, the accuracy of the evidence, or the authenticity of the situation. Flight may mean ignoring the information, disengaging from the feedback process, misinterpreting or distorting the evidence, analysis, or conclusions in ways that are favorable to and reinforce existing practices and capacities. Discrepant feedback may also alter the relationship between the learner and his partner and negatively affect the learner's openness to subsequent feedback.

When the learner is in a healthy emotional state and feels safe to acknowledge both strengths and weaknesses, the learner is more open to the feedback process. Learners who welcome feedback are those who are committed to continuous improvement, understand that feedback is a natural part of the learning process, and express a certain degree of

dissatisfaction with their current practice. This level of dissatisfaction is a signal that they are open to strengthening their practice. Carl Glickman (2002) notes, "Without the cultivation of dissatisfaction and critique, without being clear about our purposes, and without the need to use a knowledge base in practice, we have no education and no profession" (p. 6). On the other hand, when learners believe they have achieved a level of excellence with a practice, they are less interested in improvement because they have cultivated a sense of satisfaction with their work. This satisfaction promotes a greater need for protecting their current sense of identity and closes them off from engaging in a self-generated feedback process or from using feedback offered to them.

Psychologists James Prochaska, John Norcross, and Carlo DiClemente (1994) describe five stages of readiness to change (see Table 4.1). For learners to change, they must be at the *preparation* stage. Earlier stages of *precontemplation* and *contemplation* are ones

Table 4.1: **Stages of Change**

Stages	Description
Precontemplation	Denies there is a need to change; has no intention of changing; chooses not to acknowledge the situation; expresses comfort with current practice
Contemplation	Acknowledges the need to change, yet does not fully understand what needs to change, what is associated with the change, or how to make the change; emotionally unready to change
Preparation	Has a strong intention to make the change in the near future yet is lacking a detailed plan to make the changes
Action	Engages in new behavior in ways that are visible to self and others; requires time and effort
Maintenance	Redesigns routines, environment, and resources to maintain the change and prevent relapse; requires constant monitoring and assessment
Termination	Eliminates any further need for change in relationship to this specific area, practice, etc.

Source: Adapted from *Changing for good: A revolutionary six-stage program for overcoming bad habits and moving your life positively forward*. By J.O. Prochaska, J.C. Norcross, and C.C. DiClemente. Copyright 1994 James O. Prochaska, John C. Norcross, and Carlo C. DiClemente.

in which a learner has not yet demonstrated readiness to carry out change.

Neuroscience offers insights into the relationship between one's emotional and cognitive states. In his application of social neuroscience to the practice of leadership and management, David Rock (2008) explains how the brain's biological functions influence how humans relate to one another and to their experiences. In the SCARF model, Rock builds on two themes emerging from research. The first, is that the "motivation driving social behavior is governed by an overarching organizing principle of minimizing threat and maximizing reward" (p. 1). The second principle is that the human brain responds to its social needs in ways similar to its more basic human needs. The SCARF model incorporates the following five aspects of the human experience to guide leaders and managers in cultivating both the emotional and physical environment that support change:

Status	an individual's significance or importance
Certainty	one's ability to have confidence about his or her future
Autonomy	one's sense of being in control of or influence in the situation
Relatedness	one's ability to connect with and feel safe with others
Fairness	one's perception of integrity and honesty among people.

Rock (2008) explains that threats to any of these five elements produce the same responses within a person's brain that occur when one's physical safety is threatened. Learning partners who understand the impact of a learner's emotional state on his cognitive state may be better able to reduce the learner's perception of threat and increase openness to constructing knowledge. In this way, the learning partner helps the learner build knowledge that will strengthen his competence and motivation to improve. Learning partners can address the five elements with specific, authentic, and honest statements focused on the elements. Some examples are below.

- Our conversation today about your practices is designed to support you in discovering more about how you make decisions within your practice.
- My purpose today is to be your partner in learning and support you as you discover and develop a deeper understanding about your practice.
- As we talk today, you will be the driver of the conversation.
- I appreciate that you have expressed the desire to continue to refine and expand your practice.

Physical state. One's physical state influences readiness for learning primarily because it influences emotional stability and the capacity for cognitive processing. The amount of sleep, proper nutrition, adequate exercise, and overall good health affect how people perform mentally, physically, and emotionally. Diminished cognitive and metacognitive alertness are reflected in tiredness, hunger, or stress. Reporting an update on research supporting neuroleadership, Al Ringleb, David Rock, and Chris Ancona (2012) describe factors, including exercise, sleep, play time, and down time, relationship, and mindfulness, that contribute to optimal mental health. They highlight research by Jessica Payne and Elizabeth Kensinger on the impact of physical and emotional well-being on cognitive capacity. "When a person has high levels of stress and negative mood, resulting in poor sleep," they report, "the consequence will be significant cognitive impairment, affecting basic perception as well as judgment and decision-making" (p. 24).

Figure 4.1: **Johari Window**

Solicits feedback / Shares feedback

	Known to self	Not known to self
Known to others	1 **Arena:** Known to self and others	3 **Blind spot:** Known to others
Not known to others	2 **Façade:** Known to self but not known to others	4 **Unknown:** Known to neither self nor others

Source: Adapted from *Group process: An introduction to group dynamics* by J. Luft. Copyright 1984 Joseph Luft.

Cognitive state. The feedback process depends on refined cognitive and metacognitive processes. To prepare for feedback learners demonstrate two critical abilities. One is an understanding that they are open to learn and understand that they have inherent blind spots that can be illuminated through the feedback process. The second is competence in critical thinking and particularly in metacognition.

Blind spots are areas about which individuals have no information about themselves. Douglas Stone and Sheila Heen (2014) claim that a gap exists "between what we think we present and the way others see us. We may not recognize ourselves in others' feedback, even when everyone else would agree that it's the conventional wisdom about who we are and how we are" (p. 78). Developed by psychologists Joseph Luft and Harry Ingham in 1955 and first published in 1963, the Johari Window provides a model for explaining what people know and what they do not know about themselves. Figure 4.1 is a representation of the Johari Window. Each of four "windowpanes" represents what is known or unknown about a person.

Windowpane 1 represents what a person and others publicly know about him. Windowpane 2 is what a person knows about himself but others do not. Windowpane 3, the blind spot, is what others know about the person, but what the person himself does not know; this windowpane presents opportunities for gaining knowledge through the feedback process. Windowpane 4 represents what neither the person nor others know; this windowpane presents an opportunity for generating new understanding through engagement with a learning partner.

The feedback process, then, is a means through which learners both seek and share information and construct knowledge about their practice. A learning-focused feedback process illuminates what a learning partner is unable to observe and often what a learner may not know at a conscious level such as what a learner is thinking, how the learner prepared, the learner's perceptions of his practice, or what future actions a learner may be considering. The feedback process engages in exploring and analyzing both the learner's cognitive and metacognitive processes that are not visible to a learning partner.

The feedback process can also illuminate the blind spots if the learner is open to discovering them, open to examining the assumptions and beliefs that drive the actions, and open to examining specific cues that prompt various responses. This openness is a part of the readiness process. Without a willingness to seek and understand different perspectives, even when they are contrary to what is desired or expected, the learner can be neither honest with herself nor construct new knowledge with data and evidence from others.

Readiness for the feedback process includes having the cognitive capacities that facilitate *metacognition* and *reflection.* Robert Bing-You and Robert Trowbridge (2009) discuss the need for learners to develop such capacities and the consequences for failing to do so:

> Metacognition, described as thinking about one's thoughts and feelings, seems to be an important cognitive capacity for a learner to know how well he or she is performing. Reflective thinking and learning have been advocated as one component of metacognition. Evidence suggests that novice learners have poorly developed metacognitive skills such as reflection, which may lead to inflated self-appraisals and contribute to perpetual incompetence. Further study of metacognitive capabilities of physician-learners is needed. If metacognition is a requirement for development of expertise, then another reason for failing at feedback may be insufficient focus on developing such capacities. (p. 1331)

Developing the cognitive capacities for engaging in the feedback process must enter the forefront of learning about feedback. When feedback processes take place among adults in higher and professional education settings, a common misconception exists that learners who achieve adulthood are competent critical thinkers. Such competencies include understanding quality and making complex judgments. Sandler (2009) describes these capabilities as connoisseurship, "a highly developed form of competence in qualitative appraisal" (p. 57) that allows learners to develop self-regulation and exhibit expertise in making judgments about their practice and that of others (Carless, 2013). The cognitive capacities essentially are *critical analysis, evaluation,* and *knowledge building.* All are dependent on the application of critical thinking skills.

Critical analysis involves the ability to understand the expectations, observe nonjudgmentally one's own and others' practice, and seek and use evidence to make comparisons. It also includes analyzing the situative nature of practice, how the occurrence of practice within its current context impacts learner's thoughts and behaviors.

Evaluation includes using evidence, understanding of the criteria, and analyzing practice to judge practice and identify potential contributing factors. Potential contributing factors may be the learner's misconceptions; current knowledge, skill, or efficacy; situational conditions; misunderstanding of criteria; misalignment of goal and practice, among others.

The last phase of the cognitive process is developing next actions based on the evaluation and understanding of available resources necessary to support change in practice. David Nicol (2013) uses the term *reflective knowledge building* to describe the cognitive process that occurs within the feedback process:

> Strong evaluation skills are necessary if [adult] students are to be able to identify gaps in their understanding, misconceptions, discrepancies, errors, structural deficiencies, other perspectives, or weaknesses in the work they produce. Second, students must also have explicit opportunities to use the results of these evaluative processes to repair misunderstandings and to

build a better understanding. This entails knowledge building — filling knowledge gaps, restructuring current representations of content and/or creating new or modifying pre-existing mental models. Knowledge building is as important as it provides an identifiable reference point that can be used to gauge whether feedback processes have had any effect. If feedback processes do not result in any knowledge building then arguably they have had no impact. Key issues for learning here are the nature, extent, and validity of this knowledge building as well as its visibility. (p 35)

Without sufficient capacity to engage in critical analysis, a learner's ability to participate fully in the feedback process is limited. Explicit professional learning about facilitated and independent practice with expectations for application of critical analysis are pathways to refine a learner's critical thinking skills.

Learning environment

A learner's mindset and cognitive state are the internal learner attributes that influence how the learner shows up in the feedback process. A learner's readiness for the feedback process is influenced also by the organizational climate and culture in which the learner exhibits her practice. The nature of relationships with learning partners, trust, an environment that supports learning, and access to necessary supports are important factors of the learning environment that support frequent and meaningful learning-focused feedback processes.

Relationship with learning partners. A significant aspect of the learning environment is the relationship the learner has with her learning partner. Trust between and among the learner and learning partners is the bedrock upon which openness, honesty, and genuine dialogue take place. Stone and Heen (2014) confirm that a crucial responsibility for feedback rests with the learner, yet acknowledge that the learning partner has a role in cultivating the readiness of the learner to accept and use feedback. They describe three factors that influence the feedback process: the relationship that exists among learning partners, the learner's identity, and perceived truthfulness of the feedback. When both the learner and the learning partner are primed for learning, feedback leads to action.

David Carless (2013) and Jan McArthur and Mark Huxham (2013) describe feedback as a dialogic process. McArthur and Huxham, moreover, state that the concept of feedback as a dialogic process emphasizes the relationship of the learner and learning partners. They explain that dialogue is a human activity and one in which learners "flourish as humans and best achieve our potential through social immersion in, and engagement with, diverse perspectives and ideas" (p. 94). Based on Paulo Friere's (1993) theory of learning, dialogue is the means to cultivate significance as a human being. In true dialogue partners park their judgmental selves at the door and enter with openness to reconsider assumptions and beliefs and be moved by others' perspectives. Fear and self-preservation are barriers that inhibit the very purpose of dialogue. When the learning partner enters the feedback process as a master, he assumes superiority or expertise that reduces his openness to learning. When this happens genuine dialogue cannot occur. McArthur and Huxham suggest that learning partners act not as masters who declare what is right and wrong, but rather as ushers who accompany adult learners on their learning journey

proficiency, reflect on their skills, and improve as a result of their task engagement. Those with a performance goal focus are more interested in demonstrating what they know and avoiding negative perceptions or judgments. Bates et al. (2013) contend that longevity in the clerkships, relational trust among learners and their learning partners, perception of self as learner, and the complexity of the task influence learners to set learning rather than performance goals. Harold Bok, Pim Teunissen, Annemarie Spruijt, Joanne Fokkemam, Peter von Beukelen, Debbie Jaarsma, and Cees van der Vleuten (2013) note that students are "motivated to seek feedback out of a responsibility towards patients and clients, which stimulated them to seek feedback to improve their clinical competence" (p. 286). They add that the learner's interest, experience, and confidence in the topic and the learner's self-assessed knowledge and performance of a specific task stimulates or inhibits feedback-seeking behaviors. When learners undertake tasks that are relevant, challenging, and learning-focused and have known beneficiaries, they are more likely to engage in feedback processes that support their learning.

The sequence of learning tasks is another important feature affecting feedback. A premise of this book is that the purpose of feedback is learning. When learning tasks that serve as the learning objects for the feedback process are widely discrepant from one another, learners may have no opportunity to apply their learning to change practice. And when the learning tasks are too similar to one another, the newer task may not stimulate flow, so the learner perceives no benefit from the feedback process. This perception may have a negative effect on the learner's willingness to engage fully in subsequent feedback processes. When the learning tasks have some amount of overlap that allows learners to integrate

change in practice drawn from a previous feedback process, learners simultaneously apply their new learning and assess progress.

For the feedback process to have its greatest effect, both learners and learning partners must consider the nature and purpose of the task. They need to focus feedback processes on tasks they perceive to be challenging and present opportunities for learning, rather than those that are more routine. Such task selection preserves the purpose of the feedback process as a means for growth.

Conclusion

Conditions in which the feedback process occurs affect the quality of the feedback and its eventual usefulness in promoting ongoing learning and practice. Those responsible for the feedback process, both learners and their learning partners, share responsibility for creating appropriate conditions for the feedback process to have its greatest impact on both individuals and their organizations (see Tool 4.1: *Conditions of feedback*). Engaging in the feedback process with integrity, fairness, honesty, and emotional and physical well-being will contribute to strengthening the presence of the key conditions for feedback's success. Simultaneously working on strengthening the conditions to increase openness to feedback will create a feedback-rich culture in which both internally and externally generated feedback can flow continuously. One should not wait passively for the conditions to be right to engage in the feedback process, but rather to act with urgency to create the necessary conditions. It is imperative to remember there is reciprocity between the quality of the feedback process and the conditions for its effectiveness. When the feedback process is implemented with skillfulness and deep consideration for the learner's mindset, the learning environment, and the nature of the task, both the learner and the conditions improve simultaneously. Readers may use Tool 4.2: *Critical thinking defined* and Tool 4.3: *Critical thinking habits and skills* to extend the practice of critical thinking in their systems to make feedback more conducive to learning. When feedback continues to be one-way information, with judgment or evaluation as the primary role, the conditions for openness will likely be slower to develop. On the other hand, conditions for learning will more naturally evolve when feedback is a dialogic process in which learners understand expectations and have clear goals, are ready to engage fully in the feedback process, and are immersed in meaningful tasks that challenge their capacity.

Reflections

1. Of the conditions necessary for the feedback process described in this chapter, which is most significant? What are your reasons for selecting this one?

2. What other conditions, not discussed, would you add to the list? How do they influence the feedback process?

3. Analyze the conditions for feedback within your organization. Which are present? Which are not? On what evidence are you basing your analysis?

4. What are necessary steps needed within your organization to create the conditions for the feedback process?

5. Consider this statement: It is necessary to have the conditions in order for the feedback process to be effective. Explain whether you agree or disagree with this statement and why. Under what circumstances might the opposite be true?

References

Bambrick-Santoyo, P. (2012). *Leverage leadership*. San Francisco, CA: Jossey-Bass.

Bates, J., Konkin, J., Suddards, C., Dobson, S., & Pratt, D. (2013). Student perceptions of assessment and feedback in longitudinal integrated clerkships. *Medical Education, 47*(4), 362–374.

Bing-You, R.G. & Trowbridge, R. I. (2009). Why medical educators may be failing at feedback. *JAMA, 302*(12), 1330–1331. doi:10.1001.

Bok, H., Teunissen, P., Spruijt, A., Fokkema, J., van Beukelen, P., Jaarsma, D., & van der Vleuten, C. (2013). Clarifying students' feedback-seeking behaviours in clinical clerkships. *Medical Education, 47*(3), 282–291.

Carless, D. (2013). Sustainable feedback and the development of student self-evaluative capacities. In S. Merry, M. Price, D. Carless, & M. Taras (Eds.), *Reconceptualising feedback in higher education: Developing dialogue with students* (pp. 113–122). London, UK and New York, NY: Routledge.

Carless, D. (2013b). Trust and its role in facilitating dialogic feedback. In D. Boud & E. Molloy (Eds.), *Feedback in higher and professional education: Understanding it and doing it well* (pp. 90–103). London, UK and New York, NY: Routledge.

Csíkszentmihályi, M. (1997). *Finding flow.* New York, NY: Basic.

Deal, T. & Peterson, K. (2009). *Shaping the school culture: Pitfalls, paradoxes, and promises. 2nd edition.* San Francisco, CA: Jossey-Bass.

Drago-Severson, E. (2009). *Leading adult learning: Supporting adult development in our schools.* Thousand Oaks, CA: Corwin Press and Oxford, OH: NSDC.

Dweck, C. (2006). *Mindset: The new psychology of success.* New York, NY: Random House.

Freire, P. (1993). *Pedagogy of the oppressed.* New York, NY: Continuum Books.

Glickman, C. (2002). *Leadership for learning: How to help teachers succeed.* Alexandria, VA: ASCD.

Luft, J. (1984). *Group process: An introduction to group dynamics.* Palo Alto, CA: Mayfield Publishing Co.

McArthur, J. & Huxham, M. (2013). Feedback unbound: From master to usher. In S. Merry, M. Price, D. Carless, & M. Taras (Eds.), *Reconceptualising feedback in higher education: Developing dialogue with students* (pp. 92–102). London, UK and New York, NY: Routledge.

Nicol, D. (2013). Resituating feedback from the reactive to the proactive. In D. Boud & E. Molloy (Eds.), *Feedback in higher and professional education: Understanding it and doing it well* (pp. 34–49). London, UK and New York, NY: Routledge.

Payne, J.D. & Kensinger, E.A. (2011). Sleep leads to qualitative changes in the emotional memory trace: Evidence from fMRi. *Journal of Cognitive Neuroscience, 23*(6), 1285–1297.

Prochaska, J.O., Norcross, J.C., Diclemente, C.C. (2007). *Changing for good: A revolutionary six-stage program for overcoming bad habits and moving your life positively forward.* New York, NY: Morrow.

Reina, D.S. & Reina, M.L. (2006). *Trust and betrayal in the workplace: Building effective relationships in your organization, 2nd ed.* San Francisco, CA: Berrett-Koehler.

Ringleb, A., Rock, D., & Ancona, C. (2012). NeuroLeadership in 2011 and 2012. *NeuroLeadership Journal, 4,* 1–35.

Rock, D. (2008). SCARF: A brain-based model for collaborating with and influencing others. *NeuroLeadership Journal, 1,* 78–87.

Scheffer, B.K. & Rubenfeld, M.G. (2000). A consensus statement on critical thinking in nursing. *Journal of Nursing Education, 39*(8), pp. 352–359. Available at http://www.umich.edu/~elements/probsolv/strategy/ctskills.htm.

Scriven, M. & Paul, R. (1987, Summer). Critical thinking as defined by the National Council for Excellence in Critical Thinking. 8th Annual International Conference on Critical Thinking and Education Reform. [Website]. Available at www.criticalthinking.org/pages/defining-critical-thinking/766.

Stone, D. & Heen, S. (2014). *Thanks for the feedback: The science and art of receiving feedback well.* New York, NY: Penguin.

Vella, J. (2002). *Learning to listen, learning to teach: The power of dialogue in educating adults.* San Francisco, CA: Jossey-Bass.

Conditions of feedback

Use the tool below to plan for and reflect on the conditions for successful feedback processes.

Ask these questions during planning:

How will I address the conditions within the feedback process?

How will the presence or absence of any condition influence the success of the feedback process?

After the feedback process, ask:

How might I strengthen these conditions in future feedback process?

Conditions for feedback	Tactics for addressing conditions in upcoming feedback processes	Tactics for strengthening conditions in future feedback processes
Learner's mindset		
Emotional state		
Physical state		
Cognitive state		
Learning environment		
Learning partners		
Learning task		

Critical thinking defined

Because the term *critical thinking* is frequently used, many people assume they know what it means.

In a statement presented at the 8th Annual International Conference on Critical Thinking and Education Reform, Michael Scriven and Richard Paul (1987) characterized critical thinking in "its exemplary form" as "based on universal intellectual values that transcend subject matter divisions: clarity, accuracy, precision, consistency, relevance, sound evidence, good reasons, depth, breadth, and fairness" (para. 3).

Use Scriven and Paul's statement at the Foundation for Critical Thinking website:

www.criticalthinking.org/pages/defining-critical-thinking/766

1) Read the complete statement. Use the table on the next page to make notes or comments as you read.

2) Examine your own and colleagues' understanding of and beliefs about critical thinking.

3) Identify the ideas that resonate with you in some way and those with which you disagree.

4) Consider how critical thinking as described by Scriven and Paul applies to the feedback process.

Critical thinking defined

I agree with these ideas	I disagree with these ideas	How these ideas apply to the feedback process

Critical thinking habits and skills

Critical thinking is a series of cognitive processes that can be applied independently or in combination to support deepening practice with critical thinking. Use this tool to expand your understanding of and skillfulness with critical thinking within the feedback process. Barbara K. Scheffer and M. Gaie Rubenfeld (2000) offer a useful resource that describes and provides examples of critical thinking habits and critical thinking skills. Examine the habits and skills for those that are more common in your routine practice and those that you might add to your routine repertoire.

1. Analyzing	Separating or breaking a whole into parts to discover their nature, functional and relationships "I studied it piece by piece" "I sorted things out"
2. Applying Standards	Judging according to established personal, professional, or social rules or criteria "I judged it according to . . ."
3. Discriminating	Recognizing differences and similarities among things or situations and distinguishing carefully as to category or rank "I rank ordered the various . . ." "I grouped things together"
4. Information Seeking	Searching for evidence, facts, or knowledge by identifying relevant sources and gathering objective, subjective, historical, and current data from those sources "I knew I needed to lookup/study . . ." "I kept searching for data."
5. Logical Reasoning	Drawing inferences or conclusions that are supported in or justified by evidence "I deduced from the information that . . ." "My rationale for the conclusion was . . ."
6. Predicting	Envisioning a plan and its consequences "I envisioned the outcome would be . . ." "I was prepared for . . ."
7. Transforming Knowledge	Changing or converting the condition, nature, form, or function of concepts among contexts "I improved on the basics by . . ." "I wondered if that would fit the situation of . . ."

Types of Feedback

IN THIS CHAPTER Readers examine a typology of feedback along a continuum of degrees of (a) control/engagement/responsibility, (b) content, and (c) outcomes. Readers will:

- Study detailed examples of the nine types of feedback: desistance, correction, approval, attribution, evaluation, assessment, analysis, construction, and deconstruction.
- Understand how *deconstruction* deepens *construction* by applying new knowledge in different settings.
- Reflect on experiences with different types of feedback and roles that mentors, supervisors, evaluators, learning partners, and learners play.
- Use the tools to analyze current feedback practice.

The primary purpose of feedback is learning; that overriding principle guides the feedback process and focus. In its highest form, the feedback process is a dynamic, generative process that occurs during dialogue with others or oneself. The Implementation standard (see sidebar) for professional learning stresses the role of constructive feedback as a part of the process for implementing new learning. The term *constructive feedback* implies that a learner is actively engaged in constructing new knowledge and that the process is based on

Implementation Standard

Professional learning that increases educator effectiveness and results for all students applies research on change and sustains support for implementation of professional learning for long-term change.

Standards for Professional Learning, 2011, http://learningforward.org/standards/implementation#.

data and evidence drawn from learning objects or learning tasks.

The opposite of constructive feedback, nonconstructive feedback is one-way delivery of information from an external partner to a learner without engaging the learner in constructing new knowledge; consequently, it is unlikely to generate learning that will transform future practice. Some who have been traditionally givers of feedback may not be dissuaded from their current understanding or practice of feedback as static, transmitted information. Within that approach to feedback the critical attribute missing — knowledge constructed by the learner in a dialogic or a self-generated process — may prevent learning from such feedback. In fact, some learning partners who give nonconstructive feedback may believe that their feedback is constructive because they are giving the learner specific information about the learning object and may also offer direction for next actions. Yet such a practice is not confirmation of learning. A teacher might be able to restate a correction or suggestion from a supervisor, for example, yet not understand what is required to apply that correction to his practice tomorrow. Feedback is constructive only if the learner is able to construct new knowledge and apply that knowledge to subsequent practice.

This chapter does not intend to resolve the argument about whether it is necessary that all feedback be constructed within a dialogic process. It does take the stand that feedback intended for the purpose of learning must result in newly constructed knowledge that is applied to practice. To that end, the chapter presents a typology of feedback and examines the feedback process through which to achieve learning-focused feedback.

Feedback typology

This chapter proposes a typology of feedback and examines the situations in which each type might best fit. With an understanding of the types of feedback, readers are able to deepen their understanding of which types are relevant to their particular roles and be able to make better use of the feedback process.

Readers with distinctly different areas of responsibilities may find it challenging to imagine how all types of feedback are integrated into their work. In fact not all the types of feedback will be useful for everyone. For example, supervisors who are responsible for completing annual performance appraisals might employ evaluation feedback more often than other types. When supervisors assume the role of a learning partner, they may find other types of feedback more appropriate. Coaches, on the other hand, may more often use constructed feedback. Capable learners may find that they engage in self-generated feedback daily, yet have fewer opportunities for other types of feedback.

The proposed typology addresses the full range of feedback types used in both supervisory and learning situations in professional or higher education. It is grounded in a review of the literature and acknowledges that there are multiple purposes for the feedback process as well as various situations within which the process occurs and various outcomes that emerge from it. Figure 5.1 on page 47 depicts nine distinct types of feedback. The types are delineated along two shifts that occur in the feedback process. On one shift is in *responsibility* for, *control* of, and *engagement* in the feedback process. The second shift represents the *outcome* of the feedback process, that is, a shift from information to knowledge construction and use. The use of the shifts along a continuum suggests that feedback is a dynamic process that may change depending on the purpose and desired outcome. Other factors such as the learner's self-perception, the relationship between the learner and learning partner, task complexity and significance, learner's capacity for self-analysis, and the potential impact on the learner's practice influence the purpose and outcome of the feedback process, and therefore influence the shifts that occur.

For example, as learners become more skillful at self-analysis and effective in their practice, their need for different types of feedback shifts as well. The shifts along a continuum stress, too, that the learning partner plays a more dominant role in some forms of feedback and at other times places the learner at the forefront, regardless of the learning partner's level of authority, status, or expertise.

What is not included in the shifts along the continuum is the *direction* of the feedback, positive or negative. Some might perceive the types of feedback on the left side as more negative. The perception of positive or negative, however, is primarily determined by the learner

Figure 5.1: **A Typology of Feedback**

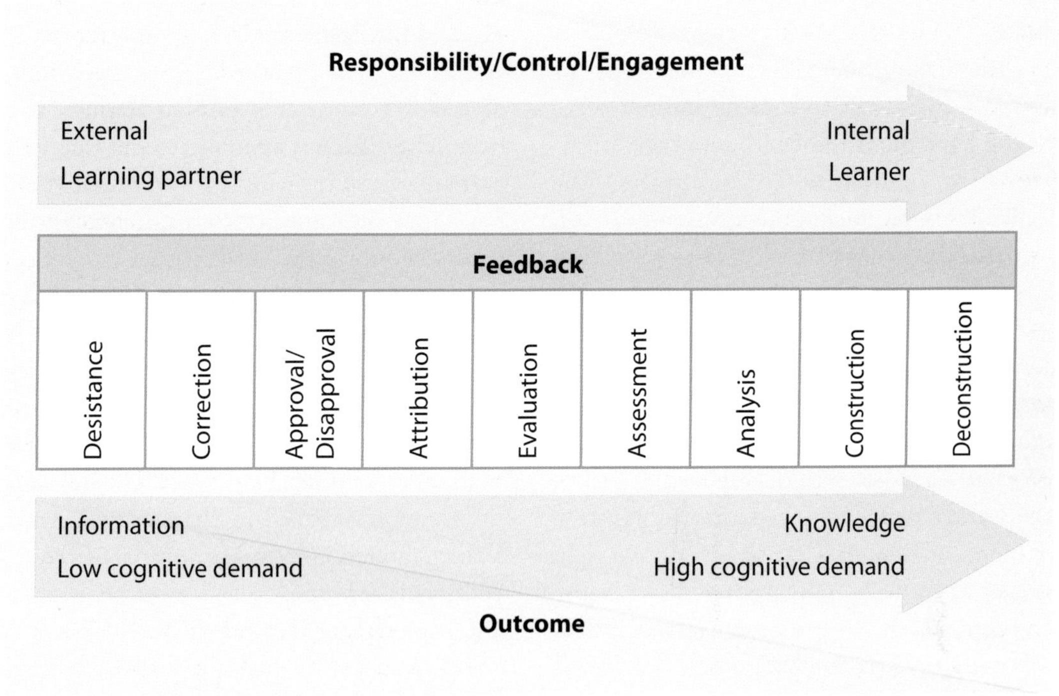

Responsibility/Control/Engagement

| External | Internal |
| Learning partner | Learner |

Feedback

| Desistance | Correction | Approval/Disapproval | Attribution | Evaluation | Assessment | Analysis | Construction | Deconstruction |

| Information | Knowledge |
| Low cognitive demand | High cognitive demand |

Outcome

and influenced by a number of factors such as the learner's relationship with the external partner (if one is present), the significance of the situation in which the practice is exhibited or from which the learning objects emerge, and the learner's mindset. Each type of feedback contains the potential for either a positive and negative learner response.

This typology builds on other continua. It offers one way to categorize and delineate multiple definitions and types of feedback appearing in existing research in K–12 education and in professional and higher education. The typology provides guidance for integrating feedback into professional learning and higher education settings. Three bodies of work informed the development of the feedback typology. One is the consultant-collaborator-coach continuum developed by Laura Lipton and Bruce Wellman (2001) in *Mentoring*

Matters: A Practical Guide to Learning-focused Relationships. The second is Carl Glickman's (2002) developmental supervision model in *Leadership for Learning: How to Help Teachers Succeed.* The third influence comes from the levels of coaching described by Dave Ellis (2006) in *Life Coaching.* Each of these models depicts a shift in responsibility from the learning partner, whether a teacher, mentor, supervisor, expert, peer, or coach, to the learner as the learner's capacity for self-analysis grows and as the role of learning is elevated. The shifts in the continuum of the feedback typology depict that there is movement along the continuum and that movement is driven by the learner's needs and the learning partner's assessment of the best way to support learning in the feedback process. While the typology distinguishes among the various types of feedback for illustrative purposes, as Tunstall and Gipp (1996) note, the types may blend together as the learning partner or learner engage in the process to address multiple topics.

The diagram delineates various types of feedback based on the content and outcome. At the left side of the continuum, the learning partner controls the feedback process. The feedback is a product at the information level, so the learner may not yet have internalized or necessarily understood it; therefore, it has less potential to shape the learner's future actions. In addition, the feedback process at the left side of the continuum requires that the learner do little cognitive processing. This form of feedback excludes opportunities for the learner to increase capacity in objective, criterion-referenced self-analysis. At the right side of the continuum requiring higher cognitive demand, the learner is more responsible for and engaged in the feedback process by actively constructing knowledge through overt (e.g. discussing with a learning partner) or covert (e.g. reflecting) processes.

The continuum remains fluid with distinct implications for each point. Within one supervisory conversation, for example, the learner may receive corrections and may also engage in self-analysis that leads to self-generated construction of new knowledge. The goal of the feedback process is to develop learner expertise and ability to construct knowledge through self-analysis. Some learners, however, need time and support to develop the capacity to do this level of cognitive work.

Desistance

On the far left of the continuum is desistance. With this type of feedback an external learning partner typically controls the feedback content and the learner exerts little cognitive processing. Sometimes desistance is generated internally by an external stimulus such as the pain produced when touching a hot object. The learner's response to desistance is often immediate. While some might not view desistance as feedback, in certain learning situations, especially clinical or live-client settings, this form of feedback is appropriate and frequent, particularly when there is an immediate need for action. In a medical setting, it might be used when an action will harm a patient. In a classroom setting, it might be helpful, too, as coaches are helping teachers respond to misbehavior that is disruptive or harmful. The message is simple, direct, unemotional, and explicit. It conveys the action to take rather than what not to do. Desistance provides static information designed to change the learner's immediate actions. The learning partner exerts control of the learner's practice and holds a clear expectation that the command will be followed.

Examples of desistance include:
• Take your hand off the student's shoulder.
• Slow down.
• Repeat that step.
• Lower your voice.

Correction

Correction informs the learner about a change needed. An external partner gives the correction based on his or her judgment of the performance of the learner. In this form of feedback the learner receives an implicit message of desistance as well as an alternative action to implement without requiring the learner to determine the action on her own. The key distinction between desistance and correction is that the learning partner draws attention to the current practice and the change needed, whereas in desistance the needed action is the only one identified. In many situations desistance and correction are blended together. As with desistance, the learning partner exerts external control in the practice of the learner and holds a clear expectation that the learning partner responds by following the correction given. Some learners may internalize the purpose of the correction, particularly if they are aware of the criteria for success, yet the learning partner makes no effort to offer any explanation for the necessary change.

Examples of correction include:
• Move from the front to the back of the room.
• Instead of talking to the whole group, speak to each student privately.
• Allow others to speak before sharing your idea.
• Complete both parts of the task rather than just the first.

Approval/Disapproval

In this type of feedback the external partner demonstrates his or her response, often based on a covert judgment, about a learner's practice by expressing approval or disapproval verbally or nonverbally. The external partner exerts control in the situation by both making a judgment and expressing either approval or disapproval, yet does not go so far as to identify the correction necessary. Approval and disapproval are conveyed in general terms with no specific information given other than the external partner's response. The learner is left guessing about what particular behavior prompted the response and the reason for it. Because the learner is expected to respond, yet has no specific information about what to change, the cognitive demand on the learner increases as does the learner's responsibility for making some change. Approval or disapproval may be conveyed through spoken or written messages or nonverbally. Examples of both follow.

Nonverbal examples of approval/disapproval include:
• Facial expressions such as smiles, frown, or glares; or
• Gestures such as head nodding or shaking, finger wagging, or high fives.

Verbal examples of approval/disapproval include:
• Good job!
• Not your best work.
• Needs improvement.
• Best yet!

Attribution

Attribution is the process of labeling or assigning a characteristic or trait to another person. Robert Kegan and Lisa Lahey (2001) assert that attribution conveys the speaker's response to something someone says or does by "making generalizations or characterizations about that person" (p. 99). They add that people doing the labeling are engaged in "the rather presumptuous activity of entitling ourselves to say who and how the other is" (p. 99). "Characterizing the other, even positively, though not necessarily provoking defensiveness does provoke a reaction: having been acted upon, we react. But characterizing our own experience, positive or negative, leaves the other informed (not formed) by our words" (p. 100).

Attribution provides more information to the learner than approval or disapproval, yet attribution bypasses the step of explaining what the behavior is and moves immediately to labeling it in general terms. For example, if a colleague notices that a co-worker has stayed late and pitched in to complete a project with a pressing deadline, the colleague might label the co-worker as helpful. The message does not convey the specific action that merited the label. For the purpose of understanding his practice and its impact on others and the environment, the label without the specific action is insufficient for constructing knowledge from the learning object. Without discussion of the specific practice, the learner may be unable to replicate or avoid it in subsequent situations.

> **Examples of attribution include:**
> - You definitely are a leader.
> - You are a novice.
> - You are so gracious.
> - I am so inexperienced.

Evaluation

Evaluation is judging usually in relationship to criteria known to both the learner and the learning partner. The primary purpose of evaluation is to judge practice rather than improve it. In many situations, however, those who use evaluation feedback assume that it will lead to improvement. This form of feedback sits at the midpoint in the continuum because it is the first time that external criteria are introduced into the process, yet it still requires low cognitive demand on the learner. The learner or learning partner use data to judge or place a value on the learner's practice. Evaluation is similar to approval or disapproval because it is general in nature, yet the presence of criteria is the distinguishing feature. In evaluation feedback the evaluator uses criteria to form judgments based on some data. This evaluation is typically a covert cognitive process so the learner does not have access to how the evaluation was determined. The evaluator communicates the judgment or rating, not how she arrived at the evaluation based on the criteria and data. Evaluations are a common form of feedback as core functions within organizations; they are part of performance

appraisals; and in nearly all education settings, they are a part of the learning process. Evaluations may lead to higher forms of feedback; alone, however, they do not necessarily guarantee that a learner will change his practice.

> **Examples of evaluation feedback:**
> - This is average work based on the criteria. I'd rate it 3 of 5.
> - Your performance is more than expected for a novice teacher. Based on the teacher performance rubric, I'd rate it meets expectations.
> - Your performance does not meet the criteria yet, although you are close to meeting three of the four criteria.
> - This report does not meet our standard for clear writing.

Assessment

This form of feedback is nonjudgmental and situates the learner in reference to criteria or expectations for success. The intent is to help learners know their current status and to alter future actions so that they are closer to the expected level of performance. Criteria for success become an important component of this type of feedback and are used to help the learner understand where his current practice lies in relationship to the criteria and how to improve it.

When learners engage in assessment alone or with a learning partner, they identify one or more learning objects, usually evidence drawn from practice, and compare them to criteria or expectations for success. This type of analysis allows the learner to understand how close or far he is from the desired level. Hattie and Timperley (2007) and others call this distance between current and ideal practice the *gap to close*. Yet, simply knowing the gap is insufficient to move the learner closer to the ideal. The analysis process must also integrate future planning and support to identify and successfully accomplish necessary changes to close the gap. And, as a result of the analysis process, the learner gains the motivation to persist in the changes.

Following assessment, the learner has information that she can apply to determine next actions, thus moving closer to building knowledge that allows her to transform both immediate and long-term practice. The clearer the criteria for success and the learning goal, the easier it is for the learner to determine which actions to take to move closer to the goal or to use suggestions from others to do so. Readers will notice that the length and specificity of the feedback examples increase with assessment. This occurs because the cognitive demand increases and the content expands to include evidence, how the evidence aligns with the criteria, and recommendations for next actions based on the criteria. Brief feedback statements are not possible at this level and above.

Examples of assessment feedback:

- The adaptations you made in the lesson as you were teaching demonstrate your responsiveness to students' learning needs. This practice is identified in Level 3 instructional practice and indicates that you are using some data from students to assess their progress and adjust your practice. In the future as you continue this practice, what other types of data might you be able to collect during an instructional setting so that you have data needed to make on-the-spot adjustments in your practice?

- During the community budget meeting you observed that three participants stood up, spoke out of turn, and interrupted others. After these incidents, you called for a break and asked to speak to the three participants in private. Based on your action and its influence on the rest of the meeting, other participants, these three participants, and you, explain where you think your action falls on the rubric of effective community leadership practices? What are other actions you might consider in the future to extend this practice?

- Your focus is on using learning outcomes to help students take responsibility for their own learning. Establishing learning outcomes falls in the instruction area of the performance standards. In ideal practice, as the performance standards state, when asked, students identify the learning outcome, respond to the I-can statements associated with it, and indicate where they are in relationship to reaching it. I asked five students near me, and all pointed to the learning outcome you had posted. Two of the five responded to at least one of the three I-can statements, yet none knew how to use the information to assess where they were in relationship to the learning outcome. Based on the evidence and the criteria, what level of practice aligns most closely with yours? Tell me about what you are considering as next actions.

- Your practice in staff and community engagement, based on data from observing you and the 360^0 survey results, is above expectation. You routinely seek input from a wide range of stakeholders before making decisions. You have three different advisory groups that are vehicles for input. You listen to, consider, and act on suggestions from others. I noticed that you implemented the new financial system, engaged the community in the strategic planning process, and have casual conversations with peers, supervisors, and subordinates. What other specific examples you would cite as evidence of your practice in this area? What are ways you are considering to refine your practice in this area?

Analysis

Analysis focuses on taking apart a learning object such as observed practice, a work product, or other source of data to understand its component parts and how those parts contribute to the overall object. It builds on assessment and leads to a clear delineation of the reasons for meeting or not meeting criteria. As with evaluation and assessment, criteria come to the forefront of the feedback process along with an opportunity to understand how the particular practice, which serves as the learning object, aligns with the criteria and the reasons for the alignment or lack of alignment. Assessment also integrates the learner's goals as an indicator of achievement for measuring progress toward the goal. This type of feedback acknowledges that the practice is not devoid of its context and emphasizes the interactions among the actors, the situation, and the environment. It examines the cause-effect relationships evident within the practice so the learner understands how she influences and is influenced by others, the situation, and the environment. It leads to deeper understanding about what prompted this particular action, and how those actions might influence future actions. While the learner has a significant role in analysis, she may not necessarily have the primary role in analysis.

Examples of analysis:

- Three factors prompted my actions. One was the number of new employees; the second was my notes from our meeting last year with new employees; and the third was my awareness of the timing of the meeting. This combination led me to put aside the agenda we prepared and focus on answering their questions instead of following the planned agenda. In the future I'll want to identify new employee needs before the meeting, if possible, so I can allocate time better.

- The negative way teachers responded to the requirements surprised me. I was aware that they looked to just a few people to serve as their spokespersons. I also didn't engage in preliminary conversations that might have helped me anticipate this type of reaction. I know teachers have been asked to make some other fairly significant changes in the last few months. I understand that when this combination of factors comes together, their response is reasonable. It means that I'll need to identify and understand more fully all the factors affecting people before deciding if additional expectations are appropriate.

- Let's look at the criteria for excellent performance in the area of decision making. When you review those criteria, I wonder what practices were evident in the meeting you held yesterday with the leadership team. I am interested in exploring what impact the practices had on you as a leader, the team's ability to engage in the decision making, the quality of the decision, the culture of share responsibility you want to create within the department, and your goal to share leadership with the team more routinely. I also wonder how you will apply your thoughts in the future.

- As I look at the description of ideal practice in the Innovation Configuration (IC) map, I am surprised to see that my routine practice is missing so many aspects. I am more a 3 than a 1 on this IC map. I don't often think about transferring responsibility to others; I gather and present the data rather than teach others how to do that. I do it to save them time, yet now I realize that I build their capacity when I teach them how to access data and analyze data. When they know how to access and analyze data, perhaps they may be likely do it more often.

Construction

In the feedback process *construction* is the development of new knowledge, something about which the learner has no previous consciousness or understanding. In essence, it is new knowledge, realization, discovery, or insight to the learner. The newly constructed knowledge may be known to others, though it was previously unknown to the learner at a conscious level. Knowledge construction unleashes potential because it makes the unknown known and equips the learner to make more informed decisions.

Construction emerges from analysis and is grounded in situated cognitive theory. This theory posits that learning is constructed and embedded within the particular activity, context, and culture in which it occurs (Brown, Collins, Duguid, 1989). Patricia Alexander (2003) describes construction of knowledge as expertise in the Model of Domain Learning, an alternative she proposes to more traditional models of expertise:

> Not only is the knowledge base of experts both broad and deep, but the experts are also contributing new knowledge to the domain. To create new knowledge, experts must be well versed in the problems and methodologies of the domain and active engaging in problem finding. These experts are posing questing and instituting investigations that push the boundaries of the domain. (p. 12)

Constructing knowledge can be facilitated by an external learning partner or self-initiated. Through evaluation, the learning partner is likely to be the provider of feedback in the form of information. In both assessment and analysis the learning partner's role becomes less prominent as the learner's responsibility and cognitive demand shift to the forefront. For the first time along the continuum, it is imperative that the learner has primary responsibility during construction. Learners simply are unable to construct knowledge without being engaged fully and deeply in the process (see examples, pp. 54–55).

Construction typically happens after the analysis of one or more learning objects and results in the learner generating a conclusion, generalization, or hypothesis based on the learning objects that will inform future actions. The conclusions, generalizations, or hypotheses become lessons that can be applied in other situations. Construction leads to increased consciousness about one's metacognitive process, or how one's thinking leads to certain behaviors. It also leads to the construction of knowledge that may be generalizable across multiple contexts. For example, when George listens fully and empathetically in a conversation with his friend Charmaine who is experiencing a personal struggle, she feels supported and more confident in her decisions. Then, later when George is listening in the same way to a work colleague who is frustrated about his supervisor, he might apply the same form of listening to help his colleague feel supported and more confident in his decision about how to handle the situation. Similarly, if George listens fully when interacting with his own supervisor who expressed disappointment in George's performance, he may understand more deeply the supervisor's viewpoint. He may also have a firmer grasp of his options for responding. As a result, George makes a more considered decision about his next actions. Future actions, then, might include ways to test the hypothesis or collect and analyze additional evidence to confirm or disprove a hypothesis or generalization within a different context.

Sometimes construction is an intuitive process that is not as dependent on overt analysis, yet when the analysis is a prerequisite of construction, a learner is able to understand more fully at a cognitive level, the basis or support for the newly constructed knowledge. Examples of construction are presented as sample generalizations, conclusions, and hypotheses a learner might develop from the examples of analysis feedback presented earlier.

Examples of construction:

Analysis feedback	Construction feedback
• Three factors prompted my actions. One was the number of new employees; the second was my notes from our meeting last year with new employees; and the third was my awareness of the timing of the meeting. This combination led me to put aside the agenda we prepared and focus on answering their questions instead of following the planned agenda. In the future I'll want to identify new employee needs before the meeting if possible so I can allocate time better.	• When I take into consideration multiple factors, such as the broader context and the circumstances that surround a particular situation, (participants' levels of expertise, their feelings and needs, the climate within the organization, and other data) and let go of control, I am more responsive and sensitive to others and am better able to adjust my desires and plans accordingly. I consider this an important practice for leaders. In future situations, I want to be more observant of the cues and factors around me and more conscious of how I am using data to make on-the-spot adjustments. I want to observe and assess the effects of my adjustments on others and the environment.
• The negative way teachers responded to the requirements surprised me. I was aware that they looked to just a few people to serve as their spokespersons. I also didn't engage in preliminary conversations that might have helped me anticipate this type of reaction. I know that teachers have been asked to make some other fairly significant changes in the last few months. I understand that when this combination of factors comes together, their response is reasonable. It means that I'll need to identify and understand more fully all the factors affecting people before deciding if additional expectations are appropriate.	• Things are not what they seem. In order to understand more deeply the extent of the negativity I observed, I want to collect information more widely and in different ways. Appointed spokespersons may not reflect everyone's view. I am also learning that taking time to have more personal conversations with teachers about their views and engaging them more deliberately in problem solving is a way that I can demonstrate my trust in their professional judgment. Most importantly, taking the time to understand the reasons for their response will help us plan how we move forward together. None of this works without their full engagement and commitment. In the future I'll plan time to be more deliberate about engaging everyone in the decision making related to new expectations or additional responsibilities.

Analysis feedback, continued	Construction feedback, continued
• Let's look at the criteria for excellent performance in the area of decision making. When you review those criteria, I wonder what practices were evident in the meeting you held yesterday with the leadership team. I am interested in exploring what impact the practices had on you as a leader, the team's ability to engage in the decision making, the quality of the decision, the culture of share responsibility you want to create within the department, and your goal to share leadership with the team more routinely. I also wonder how you will apply your thoughts in the future.	• I wanted to move quickly through this decision because I considered it relatively easy one to make. Fundamentally, today I acted in ways that are not aligned with what I say about shared leadership. At times I only see the world through my eyes. When I put myself in the shoes of the leadership team, particularly the department heads who will have a significant job implementing any decision we make, I realize that what I thought was a relatively easy decision has many more prongs that need deliberation, planning, and resources. I am more aware that it is challenging to trust those on the leadership team to be responsible and to support rather than direct as a way to demonstrate my commitment to shared leadership. I want to explore more deeply my beliefs about shared leadership that influence my actions and how those beliefs are affecting my professed desire to share leadership.
• As I look at the description of ideal practice in the Innovation Configuration (IC) map, I am surprised to see that my routine practice is missing so many aspects. I am more a 3 than a 1 on this IC map. I don't often think about transferring responsibility to others; I gather and present the data rather than teach others how to do that. I do it to save them time, yet now I realize that I build their capacity when I teach them how to access data and analyze data. When they know how to access and analyze data, perhaps they may be likely do it more often.	• I can see now that what I assumed was ideal practice falls short. I had not even considered adding these other practices as important in the data analysis process. I concentrated on saving time rather than on building capacity, yet I always say I am a leader of learning. This is an important learning for me because it has implications for many different situations. I will now consider how I can build capacity of others to be experts so that I am not limiting their ability to take on such important work on their own whenever they want to.

Deconstruction

Deconstruction expands knowledge construction (see examples, pp. 56–57). It moves the learner from familiar to unfamiliar to deepen knowledge. Based on a form of literary analysis attributed to Jacques Derrida (1976), deconstruction disputes the assumption that the structures of meaning are stable and universal. As an extension of constructing knowledge within the feedback process, deconstruction builds on construction to explore the applicability, meaning, and appropriateness of the constructed knowledge in different settings. The deconstructor searches for inconsistencies and conflicts, explores oppositions, surfaces different assumptions, and seeks to develop alternative meanings of the constructed knowledge. In essence, this approach to feedback deepens learning to the point at which the learner is able to understand how the constructed knowledge applies with different clients, settings, content, players, cultures, times, etc. More importantly, the learner comes to understand what may happen when the constructed knowledge does not apply. And that is how deconstruction deepens constructed knowledge.

Examples of deconstruction:

Construction feedback	Deconstruction feedback
• When I take into consideration multiple factors such as the broader context and the circumstances that surround a particular situation (participants' levels of expertise, their feelings and needs, the climate within the organization, and other data) and let go of control, I am more responsive and sensitive to others and am better able adjust my desires and plans accordingly. I consider this an important practice for leaders. In future situations, I want to be more observant of the cues and factors around me and more conscious of how I am using data to make on-the-spot adjustments. I want to observe and assess the effects of my adjustments on others and the environment.	• This is all making me think about what we mean by data. Usually we mean that it is something that is observable. We also say that valid and reliable data are observed by others in the same way. I consider myself to be intuitive. If I intuit something, I am likely to adjust to respond to it. My intuition isn't hard, observable data. Most people don't consider feelings or intuition data. For example, if I sense discomfort, isn't that data of some sort? I wonder if data always need to be what others and I observe. I also wonder whether adjustments are always necessary. There might be situations in which not responding might be the best action to take. Do we consider not responding a response? I wonder how redefining data as both observable and internal feelings will influence our work. I also want to examine how not responding is an intentional action in response to observed or felt data.
• Things are not what they seem. In order to understand more deeply the extent of the negativity I observed, I want to collect information more widely and in different ways. Appointed spokespersons may not reflect everyone's view. I am also learning that taking time to have more personal conversations with teachers about their views and engaging them more deliberately in problem solving is a way that I can demonstrate my trust	• What if things were as they seemed? Three people had a negative response. Instead of spending time trying to assess the accuracy of what appears on the surface, what if we put that time and effort into planning what comes next? Perhaps engagement and commitment are not always positively correlated. The desire to be engaged varies among people based on a wide range of factors. There are other motivators besides engagement. I can demonstrate my trust

Construction feedback, continued	Deconstruction feedback, continued
in their professional judgment. Most importantly, taking the time to understand the reasons for their response will help us plan how we move forward together. None of this works without their full engagement and commitment. In the future I'll plan time to be more deliberate about engaging everyone in the decision making related to new expectations or additional responsibilities. • I wanted to move quickly through this decision because I considered it relatively easy one to make. Fundamentally, today I acted in ways that are not aligned with what I say about shared leadership. At times I only see the world through my eyes. When I put myself in the shoes of the leadership team, particularly the department heads who will have a significant job implementing any decision we make, I realize that what I thought was a relatively easy decision has many more prongs that need deliberation, planning, and resources. I am more aware that it is challenging to trust those on the leadership team to be responsible and to support rather than direct as a way to demonstrate my commitment to shared leadership. I want to explore more deeply my beliefs about shared leadership that influence my actions and how those beliefs are affecting my professed desire to share leadership.	in people's professional judgment by giving them autonomy, choice, and support. If people had parameters, choices within those parameters, autonomy to choose, and needed supports to succeed, they might not all want to be engaged in setting the parameters, creating the options, and defining the supports needed. This isn't a simple process. It makes me want to examine human motivation and its role in my work. • Trust is reciprocal. If I trust others, should I not expect that they trust me to act with their best interests in mind? Acting in a way that considers the needs and feelings of others is what being a leader means to me. What we understand as the concept of shared leadership seems to differ. Tom Peters once wrote that a shared decision was a decision any single individual in an organization made when he or she had the best interests of the whole organization and colleagues in mind. There are some members of the leadership team who want me to decide. They'd rather not be engaged in the decision making process. Their lack of engagement does not dampen their commitment to the success of the work. The difference in these situations may rest less with the level of engagement and more with the type of issue, problem, or decision we face. It may also rest with different individual's perception of their role. It may also rest with the degree of reciprocal trust in the leader's professionalism and credibility and in the leader's trust of others.
• I can see now that what I assumed was ideal practice falls short. I had not even considered adding these other practices as important in the data analysis process. I concentrated on saving time rather than on building capacity, yet I always say I am a leader of learning. This is an important learning for me because it has implications for many different situations. I will now consider how I can build capacity of others to be experts so that I am not limiting their ability to take on such important work on their own whenever they want to.	• I am curious about whether capacity building as the driver for my actions can ever cause overload, overwhelm, or even spur resistance. I can imagine situations in which people are grateful that they don't have to know how to access and analyze data. It simply is one less thing for them to worry about. I wonder what circumstances might make it OK not to know how to work with data at this level?

Figure 5.2 summarizes the typology of feedback.

Figure 5.2: **A Summary of the Typology of Feedback**

Desistance	Correction	Approval/ Disapproval	Attribution	Evaluation	Assessment	Analysis	Construction	Deconstruction
Commands from an external learning partner to end a particular practice immediately without explanation; used when the learner, the learners' clients, or the circumstances require immediate response	Direction from an external learning partner about a necessary change in practice with the inclusion of the desired practice and no explanation; used when the learner, the learners' clients, or the circumstances require immediate change in a practice	Verbal or nonverbal message of approval or disapproval from an external partner typically based on the partners' judgment of the learner's actions and without explanation of the external partner's response	Abstract label placed on the learner based on perception or judgment of the learner's effort, quality of work, or personal characteristics; may be generated by an external learning partner or the learner	Judgment about the quality or accuracy of the learner's practice; typically is based on criteria known to the learner and learning partner; may be generated by an external learning partner or the learner	Progress monitoring or measuring based on identification of the gap between current practice and ideal practice; measurement of the gap between current practice and ideal practice using criteria for ideal practice	Examination of evidence of current status and criteria of successful practice to understand the interrelationships among the players, context, content, and to identify specific action necessary to move closer to ideal practice	Knowledge generated through analysis of practice based on goals, criteria, and evidence; uses the knowledge constructed to formulate conclusions, generalizations, or hypotheses to specify possible applications of the newly constructed knowledge to future situations	Reexamination of knowledge through a process of proposing and considering different contexts, meanings, opposites, inconsistencies, and other variances within newly constructed knowledge and deliberation about how any differences might affect the newly constructed knowledge

Evaluation · Learning

Internal control requiring response over time

External control requiring immediate response

Learning partner responsibility · Learner responsibility

Information · Knowledge

Roles in feedback process

How learners and their learning partners apply the types of feedback often depends of the situation in which feedback occurs. Figure 5.3 depicts some typical learning partner roles in educator development and displays the types of feedback those in the roles might use most often. It is important to note that the diagram is not intended to convey that only mentors, for example, use desistance and correction, just that they are more likely to do so. Depending on their context and situation, learners and learning partners may assume roles among any of the feedback types as they make the shifts in responsibility. With the desire and capacity to do so, any learner or learning partner is able to apply the highest levels of feedback in nearly every situation.

Conclusion

While nearly all feedback has the capacity to alter practice, not all feedback meets the definition proposed in this book. Learning-focused feedback is a dynamic, dialogic process that uses evidence to engage a learner, internally or with a learning partner, in constructing knowledge about practice and self. Not all situations require the same type of feedback. Some clearly require desistance or correction; others require evaluation. Understanding the different feedback types gives the learner and learning partner the ability to choose which type is appropriate in which situation (see Tool 5.1: *Analysis of current feedback practice*). When they choose learning-focused feedback, the types that begin with analysis and move to deconstruction, they commit to shifting away from more traditional approaches to feedback to the kind of feedback that shifts responsibility to the learner and increases the learner's cognitive demand. Learning-focused feedback requires that the learner take primary responsibility for learning and that the learning partner yield control. The next chapter describes the process for learning-focused feedback.

Figure 5.3: **Typical Learning Partner Roles in Education and their Alignment to Types of Feedback**

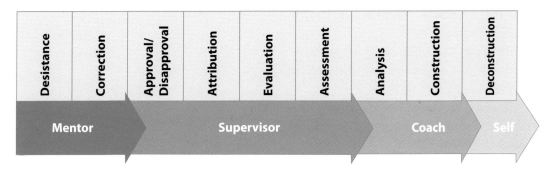

Reflections

1. What is your response to the typology presented? Explain your response.

2. What challenged you as you examined the typology? How might you resolve the challenge(s)?

3. Analyze your routine practice of feedback using the typology framework. Where does responsibility typically lie? What is the most frequent content? What is the most common outcome? Given this analysis, what changes might you want to make?

4. What's missing in the typology that you expected to see or wanted to see? How would you integrate that factor into the typology? If it cannot be integrated, explain what a new typology would look like that would include it.

5. How does the continuum help you deepen your understanding of feedback as a process of constructing knowledge?

References

Alexander, P. (2003). The development of expertise: The journey from acclimation to proficiency. *Educational Researcher, 22*(8), pp. 10–14.

Brown, J.S., Collins, A., & Duguid, P. (1989). Situated cognition and the culture of learning. *Educational Researcher, 18*(1), 32–42.

Derrida, J. (1976). *Of grammatology.* (G.C. Spivak, Trans.). Baltimore, MD, London, UK: The Johns Hopkins University Press.

Ellis, D. (2006). *Life coaching: A manual for helping professionals.* Norwalk, CT: Crown House Publishing.

Glickman, C. (2002). *Leadership for learning: How to help teachers succeed.* Alexandria, VA: ASCD.

Hattie, J. & Timperley, H. (2007). The power of feedback. *Review of Educational Research, 77*(1), 81–112.

Kegan, R. & Lahey, L. (2001). *How the way we talk can change the way we work.* San Francisco, CA: Jossey-Bass.

Lipton, L. & Wellman, B. (2001). *Mentoring matters: A practical guide to learning-focused relationships.* Sherman, CT: Miravia.

TOOL 5.1

Analysis of current feedback practice

Use this tool to examine your current feedback practice and make plans to refine it:

   a) Estimate the percentage of your current feedback in each feedback typology.
   b) Cite examples where you are most often use the types of feedback.
   c) Consider your current practice and role.
   d) Determine your desired percentage of each feedback type.
   e) Cite potential applications for the changes.

Types of Feedback	Current percentage of feedback practice	Examples	Desired percentage of feedback practice	Potential applications
Desistance				
Correction				
Approval/ Disapproval				
Attribution				
Evaluation				
Assessment				
Analysis				
Construction				
Deconstruction				

Practice with feedback types

This tool will help increase your familiarity with the nine types of feedback.

You may use the scenarios below or create your own. Select one or more to practice constructing all nine types of feedback. For example, you may use Scenario #3 to write three types and a different scenario to write other types.

Scenario #1	A novice principal is improving her ability to be visible in classrooms to support teachers as they are applying the school's newly adopted Positive Behavior Interventions System. She is finding it difficult to keep her commitment to be in some classrooms everyday and to giving weekly updates to the faculty about what she is seeing.	
Scenario #2	A veteran teacher has been challenged with the district's new science curriculum for middle grade students. As one of two science teachers in the school, he understands how critical it is that he implements the curriculum as it is written, yet in some cases he needs to revamp his long-standing and successful lesson plans.	
Scenario #3	The school's counselor is committed to serving and supporting families, and unfortunately she is making difficult choices each day to provide support to families or students. Her belief is that if she invests in supporting families, students will benefit and she often places priority on family services and supports.	
Scenario #4	The district coach for mathematics provides services to all 10 elementary schools. She runs all day from school to school to school to meet the growing demands of principals and teachers. She wants to have a better way to prioritize services beyond first-come-first-serve, yet she is finding it difficult to transition to something that might have deeper and more sustained impact.	
Scenario #5	The building leadership team meets regularly and all members express commitment to the school improvement process. To date, the team has not had been able to confront its own assumptions about student academic success. Their time is focused more on management concerns rather than student achievement.	

Feedback Process

(6)

IN THIS CHAPTER

Readers examine details about the 10 components of the learning-focused feedback process and several variations. Readers will:

- Engage deeply with the components and roles of learners and learning partners in different types of feedback processes.
- Consider prompts for different types of learning situations.
- Reflect on experiences with feedback.
- Use the tools to determine their usage of the feedback process and consider steps to strengthen their practice of the feedback process.

Feedback is a dialogic process that results in the construction of knowledge useful to the learner. The process matters both in how it engages the learner and contributes to the learner's achieving desired changes. How the feedback process unfolds depends on choices the learner and learning partner make. Sometimes the feedback process can be free flowing without a particular underlying structure; however, the use of a map or framework to guide the process increases the efficiency and results.

This chapter describes the components and sequence of the feedback process and offers some tools to guide it. Developing skills to conduct and complete the sequence of the feedback process occurs over time with practice. With a clear process map and tools to use, learners and learning partners can develop such expertise. This book offers several resources that learners and their learning partners can best use not as mindless recipes, but rather as opportunities

to deliberate about which components and sequence make sense in each unique situation. Because situations in which the feedback process occurs differ, no one approach is appropriate for all. Some core components of the feedback process, however, must be present to achieve the higher levels of feedback, and this chapter discusses those core components. In addition, this chapter also includes an explanation about the most frequently missing component of the feedback process — feedback about the process itself.

Feedback process

The feedback process presented here contains core components synthesized across multiple processes described in the literature and incorporates the critical missing component, feedback to the learning partner or learner on the feedback process. This feedback process depicts the flow within a feedback conversation that is useful to both a learner and a learning partner as they are learning how to engage in the feedback process. Once they are skillful, the process takes on the attributes of genuine dialogue in which ideas build on the perspectives shared, flowing from topic to topic as assumptions are identified and examined, and ends in using the dialogue to fuel the construction of new knowledge and future action. The process map in Figure 6.1 is a tool that includes key features for either an internally or externally driven feedback process for the purpose of promoting growth and learning.

The learner's defined outcomes guide the feedback process. The overarching outcome is construction of new knowledge and its subsequent deconstruction to examine variations in its meaning, application, and appropriateness

Figure 6.1: **Components in the Feedback Process**

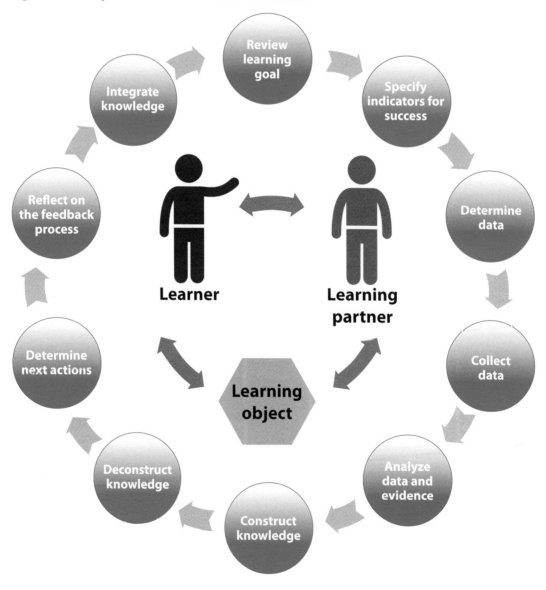

in diverse settings. In light of such a complex outcome, the feedback process cannot produce instant outcomes or results. When learners and learning partners distort the feedback process from a process of observing, analyzing, learning, applying, and reflecting into one that produces results in a matter of minutes, they will be disappointed. Committing to the feedback process builds capacity and consciousness of the choices within each decision about practice. It means development of a stronger ability to choose and control one's actions, achieve potential, and maintain a healthy self-image (Langer, 1989).

Figure 6.1 on page 64 represents the feedback process as a circle to depict a continuous process. Because a feedback process can be either internally or externally facilitated, a learner is not bound by time, schedules, or availability of learning partners to engage in the process.

Although its underlying structure is linear, this process is fluid and recursive (see Table 6.1). As learners make choices within a component, they may want to revisit a previous one. That recursiveness will then alter each subsequent move. Over time, a learner internalizes the process and develops expertise with the feedback process.

Ideally, this process leads to the highest levels of feedback — the construction and deconstruction of new knowledge, planning for use of the new knowledge, and reflection on the feedback process. Not all feedback types require learners to engage in the full process. On the

Table 6.1: **Learning-focused Feedback Process**

Components	Descriptions
Review goal and expectations.	Establish or review and clarify understanding of learning goals, expectations, and criteria of success.
Specify indicators for success.	Define what success looks like or identify which criteria will be used as a reference for assessing the effectiveness of practice.
Determine data.	Identify what data are needed for the feedback process.
Collect data.	Collect multiple forms of evidence from authentic practice or appropriate simulations.
Analyze data and evidence.	Use data and evidence to analyze practice and assess it against specified criteria to identify current status in relationship to the criteria; reflect on strengths and areas for continued focus; clarify expectations or criteria for success if necessary.
Construct knowledge.	Reflect on practice, data, and evidence from practice and analyze them to generate conclusions, generalizations, or hypotheses to apply to future practice.
Deconstruct knowledge.	Examine variations of the newly constructed knowledge to explore its appropriateness in alternative contexts.
Determine next actions.	Identify and prioritize next steps based on the new knowledge and support needed to apply it in subsequent practice.
Reflect on the feedback process.	Assess the usefulness, rigor, effectiveness of the feedback process and the contributions of learning partners.
Integrate knowledge.	Apply new learning/knowledge in subsequent actions.

Table 6.2: **Components of Feedback Process by Types of Feedback**

Components of feedback process	Typology of Feedback								
	Desistance	Correction	Approval/ Disapproval	Attribution	Evaluation	Assessment	Analysis	Construction	Deconstruction
Review learning goal.						X	X	X	X
Specify indicators for success.				X	X	X	X	X	X
Determine data.					X	X	X	X	X
Collect data.	X	X	X	X	X	X	X	X	X
Analyze data and evidence.					X	X	X	X	X
Construct knowledge.							X	X	X
Deconstruct knowledge.							X	X	X
Determine next actions.		X				X	X	X	X
Reflect on feedback process.								X	X
Integrate knowledge.								X	X

left side of the continuum, feedback types such as correction, evaluation, or even assessment, do not use the full feedback process (see Table 6.2). It is possible to apply a portion of the feedback process to traditional feedback such as when a coach presents information to the learner and asks questions that prompt reflection. For a full feedback process, one consistent with the definition of feedback presented in this text, to occur, however, the learner, often with the support of a learning partner, must *engage* in constructing and deconstructing new knowledge, reflecting on the feedback process, and integrating the new knowledge into practice. The last component of integration leads back to the first component in the feedback process, establishing new goals, and the process repeats itself.

The learning-focused feedback process leads to transformation as a result of learning. Sometimes, however, the purpose of feedback is something other than transformation; thus, the feedback giver employs types of feedback on the left side of the typology.

Cognitively demanding forms of feedback, those toward the right side of the continuum, integrate more components of the feedback process, shift responsibility to the learner, and achieve construction and deconstruction of new knowledge. Each type of feedback uses data in some way, although those data are descriptions of practice, not analysis of practice. Beginning with "Evaluation" and moving along the continuum to the right, the feedback process includes some level of analysis, ranging from a low level of internal analysis done by a learning partner alone to a higher-level analysis requiring greater engagement of a learner.

While each type of feedback could include the learner's reflection on the feedback process and integrating new knowledge, those components are often missing from traditional feedback models. When feedback is thought of as a **product** rather than a **process,** seeking input on the feedback is unnatural. In addition, the learner, the recipient of feedback, is rarely in a relationship that permits or encourages him

Table 6.3: **Components of Feedback Process by Roles**

Components of feedback process	Learner alone	Learning partner alone	Shared between a learner and learning partner
Review learning goal.	X	X	X
Specify indicators for success.	X	X	X
Determine data.	X	X	X
Collect data.	X	X	X
Analyze data and evidence.	X	X	X
Construct knowledge.	X		X
Deconstruct knowledge.	X		X
Determine next actions.	X	X	X
Reflect on feedback process.	X	X	X
Integrate knowledge.	X		

to provide feedback to the feedback giver. A common practice when feedback is viewed as a product is checking how well the learner understands the feedback. This practice is based on the assumption that if the learner understands the message, he will be more motivated to act on it. For example, a mentor who is giving correction would rarely ask the learner for feedback on the feedback process. Again, beginning with "Evaluation" on the continuum, the learner occasionally may reflect on the feedback process. The frequency of reflection or checking for learner understanding increases as the type of feedback moves to the right on the continuum.

Finally, most feedback givers consider their work completed when they have delivered their message. So, they do not consider the component of checking back with the learner to find out how she is integrating the information transmitted. This omission occurs in more traditional applications of feedback when the feedback is part of a formal performance appraisal or when feedback is not a core part of a learning process.

Those new to the feedback process are likely to begin to apply it gradually as they grow more comfortable. Supervisors or coaches may begin by ensuring that they review learning goals and ways to collect data. As these are more prevalent in their feedback work, they may generate ways to collect data with the learner. Table 6.3 depicts which components of the feedback process may be accomplished by a learner alone, facilitated by a learning partner, or shared between a learner and learning partner. The table may be useful in guiding learners and learning partners in determining how to share responsibility throughout the feedback process.

Each component guides the learner, with or without a learning partner, through the feedback process. Prompts may be in the form of invitations for thinking or questions, which learners and learning partners use to initiate the thinking that each step requires. Questions to prompt the learner through the feedback process appear in Table 6.4 on pages 68–69.

Table 6.4: **Learning Partner Prompts for the Feedback Process**

Components	Learning partner invitations	Learning partner questions
Review learning goal.	Let's review your learning goal.	• What is your learning goal?
Specify indicators for success.	Tell me about the criteria for success.	• What does it look like when you achieve your goal? • What criteria are you using for success?
Determine data.	Let's consider what types of data to collect, what sources to collect it from, and how much is appropriate.	• What types of data should we collect and examine? Quantitative, qualitative, or both? • What are ways you'd like me to collect data? • How can we be sure to get multiple sources of data? • From which sources should we collect data? Selected ones, all, randomly selected ones? • From how many different situations should we examine data? • How much data do you want? • What are the advantages or disadvantages of having these data? • How will these specific data help us analyze practice?
Collect data.	No prompts needed	• No prompts needed
Analyze data and evidence.	Here are the data I collected. I am eager to see the data you collected. Let's examine these data together, consider other data we have and combine it with other data or evidence we have to make sense of it. I also wonder about the interrelationship among those involved, the setting, context, and you and how these factors influenced this situation.	• What do you observe in these data? What patterns, themes, or outliers do you notice? • What do these data mean to you? • What other related data do you have? • To what degree are those data consistent with these? What might be some reasons for that? • How do the data connect to become evidence? • What does the evidence say about how you are doing in relationship to your goal and indicators for success? • What particular aspects of the evidence support your thinking? • Based on the evidence and your practice overall, what are your strengths in this area? • In what aspects do you want to continue to refine your efforts to engage students? • How did all the factors in this situation interact and influence each other?
Construct knowledge.	I'd like to know what you are learning, what conclusions or generalizations you are forming.	• What is clearer to you now? • What are you learning? • What do you understand now that you didn't understand as clearly before? • How will this learning influence future actions? • What is a single-sentence conclusion that represents your learning? • If you wanted to test whether this conclusion held true, what would be the hypothesis you want to test?

Components	Learning partner invitations	Learning partner questions
Deconstruct knowledge.	I want to explore when this learning might not be true and how it might vary under different circumstances. Let's examine its application in various, diverse situations.	• Under what circumstance might this conclusion not be true or this learning not be appropriate? • How do variations in the actors and the context affect this conclusion? • How might someone with less or more experience view this conclusion?
Determine next actions.	I am curious about what you are considering as next steps, how you will go about that, and what resources and support you want.	• What are ways you can continue to refine your practice? • What do you want to learn and practice? • How might you accomplish that? What is your plan to do this? • What comes first, second, third? What is your timeline? • What resources and support do you want to accomplish this plan?
Reflect on feedback process.	I am eager to strengthen my work as a learning partner. You can help me do that by sharing your perspective with me on my role in this feedback process. I am eager to know what was helpful to you and how it was helpful. I am also eager to know what wasn't helpful and your thinking about that. I'd also appreciate your suggestions on how I might alter my practice to be more effective.	• In what ways did my engagement with you support and/or hinder your learning? • What suggestions do you have for me so that I can refine my practice as a learning partner? • What did I do that helped you as a learner? How did it help? • What did I do as a learning partner that was not helpful? What make that unhelpful? • What might be a way to be more helpful as a learning partner? • What do you wish I had done that I didn't do?
Integrate knowledge.	I look forward to you sharing with me how you are using this knowledge. I'll check in with you next week.	**Asked after implementation:** • How did you integrate what you learned? • What effects did it have on you, your clients, and the context in which you applied your learning? • How will you continue to refine your practice emphasizing this new knowledge?

Table 6.5 shows an example of prompts used during the feedback process in a specific situation. In this case, a teacher is working with her coach to refine her practice in student engagement.

Table 6.5: **Prompts for Feedback Process of a Specific Learning Situation**

Components	Learning partner invitations	Learning partner questions
Review learning goal.	Your learning goal is that 100% of your students engaged at least 80% of the time in math.	• Let's review your learning goal, the expectations, and the criteria for success.
Specify indicators for success.	Let's look at the teacher performance rubric to review what the most accomplished practice looks like in this area.	• What does it look like when you achieve your goal?
Determine data.	I'll want to have some data for you to use in our feedback process. I want to know what your ideas are about the data that will be most helpful and how you want me to collect it.	• What are ways you'd like me to collect evidence about student engagement? How can we be sure to get multiple sources of evidence? What would the best kind of evidence look like? Quantitative or qualitative? How much evidence do you want? Certain students or the whole class? From one class or several?
Collect data.	No prompts needed	• No prompts needed
Analyze data and evidence.	Here are the data I collected during the last three observations. From these data, I can estimate that 90% of your students were engaged in math 70% of the time. Engagement was higher on the second day and lower on the third day. You didn't quite make your goal, yet you came close to it. Perhaps I didn't understand engagement in the same way you do. I consider students engaged when they are producing work that is associated with the learning target. As a result I didn't count the students who were reading independently as engaged in your lesson.	• What do the data say about how you are doing in relationship to your goal, the expectations, and the criteria for success? What particular aspects of the data support your thinking? Based on the data and your practice overall, what are your strengths in this area? In what aspects do you want to continue to refine your efforts to engage students? • Let's review your goal, the expectations, and criteria for success to specify what you want.

Components	Learning partner invitations	Learning partner questions
Construct knowledge.	I'd like to know what you are learning, what conclusions or generalizations you are forming about the relationship among the elements we have discussed — teaching decisions, student engagement, and student learning.	• What is clearer to you now about student engagement? What is clearer to you now? • What are you learning about how teaching decisions influence students' engagement? • How does student engagement influence their learning? • What do you understand now that you didn't understand as clearly before about the connection among teaching, student engagement, and their learning? • If you were to summarize in a single sentence a conclusion about student engagement from our work together, what would it be?
Deconstruct knowledge.	I want to explore when learning might not fit and how it might look under completely different circumstances. Let's examine its application in these situations — learners who are underachieving, high-performing students, second language learners, and students with disabilities. I'd also like to know if the content area influences the applicability of this new knowledge. Share your thoughts with me.	• How well does your conclusion about student engagement apply when you are dealing with diverse learners such as low- and high-achieving students, second language learners, or students with disabilities?
Determine next actions.	Tell me about the next steps you will take related to refining your practice with engaging students to promote their learning and what I can do to support you as you do this.	• How will your learning influence future actions?
Reflect on feedback process.	I'd like your perspective on how I can be a better learning partner and how we can refine the feedback process.	• What are your thoughts about how I can strengthen my practice as a learning partner and how we can refine the use of the feedback process?
Integrate knowledge.	I look forward to you sharing with me how you are using this information in subsequent lessons. I'll check in with you next week. **Asked after implementation:** Tell me what is changing now that you are integrating your learning.	• When might I check in with you to learn how you are integrating what you are learning in subsequent lesson? **Asked after implementation:** • How is your application of the learning going? How is it affecting your students' engagement? How does their increased engagement affect your teaching?

Table 6.6 shows a learner's application of the feedback process.

Table 6.6: **Example of a Learner's Self-generated Feedback Process**

Components	Learner reflections
Review learning goal.	My learning goal — what I want to become more skillful at — is gathering data available to me in the moment, processing the data, and using those data to make decisions about my actions.
Specify indicators for success.	One criterion of a successful facilitator is the ability to make responsive adjustments during a meeting. This means that a facilitator must be able to process cues from participants about their physical and psychological comfort, engagement, and commitment. It means being able to observe without interpretation or judgment. It means checking in with people and checking out assumptions and inferences. It means remaining neutral to the topic and focusing on the safety of people and the process.
Determine data.	I want to note when I am aware of cues and think about how I am processing those cues, choosing what actions to take, and the effects of my decisions on those I am facilitating, their work, and the situation. It will be difficult to take lots of notes, so I'll take a few index cards with me to make brief notations on including the time, who is speaking, the topic, what I am feeling, and what I perceive others are doing.
Collect data.	Note cards are available for recording information.
Analyze data and evidence.	There were three times I made notes on the cards. One was when I had finished check-in and realized that there were two people who came in late and hadn't checked in. I circled back to them. Another time was when we were reviewing the purpose of the meeting and I noticed some side conversations. I invited participants to add additional agenda items. I wasn't sure we'd get to others in the meeting, yet I wanted to be open to their input. Then there was one when I knew things were not going well and I am pretty clear about what I did — nothing intentional to refocus the meeting, yet I am not sure that I noticed any cues that might have prompted the shift in the meeting or in me. I was uncomfortable. At one point I seemed to lose control of what was going on. People were jumping in and raising ideas unrelated to the purpose of the meeting. It just spiraled from there. I felt paralyzed and now realize that there were so many things I could have done. I wish I had a parking lot to record their ideas, or taken a pause and asked them to write down everything they were thinking about or worried about so we could have organized them into related and unrelated issues. I could have used a panel of the different perspectives to air them and invite people to respond in small groups. There are so many strategies I have used before and didn't in this meeting. I want to think about the people there, the issue being discussed, and the context for clues. The people were department heads who will be responsible for implementing these communities of practice. Not all of them have been supportive of this move. Some want to be told what they are supposed to discuss and how to do that, but that is a violation of the fundamental principles of a community of practice. Willingness and openness are fundamental to the success of every community of practice. The topic is something I care deeply about. I firmly believe that expertise rests

Components	Learner reflections
Analyze data and evidence. *continued*	within each community if the community is willing to open their minds, seek knowledge they need, and learn from one another's experience and perceptions. I was probably frustrated that not everyone sees the value of communities of practice as I do. The situation was challenging because the timeline is tight; these leaders have a meeting next week; and I wanted they to be confident and ready to make their first meeting a success. I do know I was frustrated with my apparent frozen state, especially since I know a dozen or more easy techniques to pull out and use without much preparation. My conclusion is that I got caught up in the content and lost track of the facilitation process because my own interests overrode my role as a facilitator.
Construct knowledge.	There are three big lessons for me from this experience that will influence what I do in the future. First, being completely neutral is challenging, even with the best of intentions. Second, being conscious of how my personal interests, preferences, and beliefs are influencing my role as a facilitator is essential. Third, I need to be honest with others and myself when I am aware that I am unable to be fully neutral. That might mean acknowledging it to the group, stepping out of the role, or excusing myself from the conversation or meeting. While I think I was told that neutrality is an important attribute of a facilitator, I know this now on a much deeper level. I now know that acting on my lack of neutrality is my professional responsibility and ethically important to do because of the potential I have to bias a group's thinking.
Deconstruct knowledge.	Now I am wondering if there are times when being honest about my point of view is always the appropriate thing to do. There are groups that never have the opportunity to have a facilitated conversation to air their diverse perspectives and gain a deeper appreciation for one another's points of view. Even though my personal preferences might be more closely aligned with one view over another, I have the skills and techniques to allow an honest and balanced exchange of information. I am playing with the idea that my skillfulness can trump my personal beliefs in some situations.
Determine next actions.	I want to continue gaining greater awareness of how I perceive participants' cues, how I use them, and how the decisions I make influence participants, their work, and me. I want to seek other data from an experienced facilitator who can help me increase my awareness and consciousness by inviting a colleague to observe me in action. I want to test my alternative hypothesis in some way, perhaps talk about it with colleagues and participants to gather their perspectives.
Reflect on feedback process.	This was challenging to do — sitting and writing out my monologue, yet it gave me greater insight to what I was thinking. I wish I had planned to include the perceptions of others in this process. I am aware that it is easy to say what I agree with and difficult to state what isn't comfortable. Yet the exercise of disagreeing with myself helps me broaden my perspective.
Integrate knowledge.	I facilitated a meeting about a topic I have a point of view about. I asked participants to tell me if they perceived that any action I took was unfair to anyone and if I was balancing opportunities for everyone to share her perspective. I collected data on an anonymous survey at the end. No one said anything in the meeting, yet one survey suggested that I did cut short one speaker. I remember doing that now. Having these data are so important so that I can grow more aware of my actions.

The feedback process is comprehensive and may appear time consuming, yet with practice and fluency, it can become a thoughtful opportunity to examine practice with the goal of learning, can be accomplished in a brief period of time, and can be internalized so that it occurs continuously. As both learners and learning partners understand the process, use it repeatedly, and grow comfortable with it, it will be routine and fluid. Readers may examine their own familiarity with the feedback process by using Tool 6.1: *Current use of the feedback process* and Tool 6.2: *Feedback process in simulated situations or live experiences.*

Conclusion

The feedback process, when used completely, guides learners to move to the far right side of the continuum. As a defined process that scaffolds learners' and learning partners' interactions accompanied by tools, it facilitates and supports the transformation of feedback from one-way, product-oriented information to a dialogic, dynamic, internally or externally generated process. Learners engage in the feedback process independently or with learning partners. To apply the processes independently learners must observe their own behaviors and those of others with whom they interact and engage through a nonjudgmental lens and with the intent to learn. Supervisors might use these processes in formal performance reviews or in informal, formative feedback conversations with individuals or teams to increase engagement in and responsibility for learning. Colleagues might also use the process as a means to assist their peers in expanding their practice. Coaches and mentors use the process to facilitate learning for those they serve. When used within a dialogic or self-generated process, the feedback process guides learners and their learning partners in structuring their interactions to achieve desired learning goals.

Reflections

1. The feedback process described at the beginning of the chapter includes multiple components, some of which appear infrequently in traditional feedback. Identify the components that will be most challenging for learners and learning partners to integrate into their practice and suggest tactics to support their use.

2. Apply the complete feedback process to a situation you want to analyze more deeply.

3. The chapter includes a variety of feedback processes. Compare and contrast them based on potential for changing practice, ease of use, and impact on learner's capacity to engage in independent application of the feedback process.

4. To apply the feedback processes described in this chapter as a learner and a learning partner, what skills will you need to tune up and what assumptions will you need to review to develop expertise with the process?

5. Identify a specific situation in which you might apply the various feedback processes described in the chapter. In what types of situations might you not use each?

References

Langer, E. (1989). *Mindfulness.* Cambridge, MA: Da Capo Press.

Nestel, D., Bello, F., & Kneebone, R. (2013). Feedback in clinical procedural skills simulations. In D. Boud & E. Molloy (Eds.), *Feedback in higher and professional education: Understanding it and doing it right* (pp. 140–157). New York, NY: Routledge.

TOOL 6.1

Current use of the feedback process

Consider your familiarity and comfort with the feedback process. Which steps are ones you frequently use when engaged in feedback and which are new to you? What might you consider doing to refine the components you are already using? What might you do to begin implementing those components that are new to you?

Feedback process components	Currently using		Ideas for strengthening/initiating
	Yes	No	
Review learning goal.			
Specify indicators for success.			
Determine data.			
Collect data.			
Analyze data and evidence.			
Construct knowledge.			
Deconstruct knowledge.			
Determine next actions.			
Reflect on feedback process.			
Integrate knowledge.			

TOOL 6.2 *page 1 of 2* Feedback process in simulated situations or live experiences

Use this map to implement the feedback process in simulated or real situations such as laboratory experiences or classroom observations.

Step	Description	Sample prompts	Your prompts
Presimulation or observation	a. Prepare the learner for the feedback process.	a. Let's get ready for tomorrow when I'll observe you coaching a novice teacher. What do you understand is the process we'll follow?	
	b. Clarify the learner's readiness for the simulation or observed actions.	b. What have you done to prepare the teacher and yourself for my observation of your coaching?	
	c. Explore the learner's feelings about the situation.	c. How are you feeling about the upcoming observation?	
	d. Discuss potential challenges the learner may face and how the learner might respond if the challenges arise.	d. What are some challenges you anticipate might arise in this coaching situation and how will you handle them if they occur?	
	e. Clarify the learner's goals for the experience.	e. Let's review what your goal is for this coaching situation. What do you anticipate the teacher's is? How did that influence your goal?	
	f. Clarify the type of notes the learning partner will share with the learner.	f. As I observe this coaching situation, I plan to take notes. What particular areas would you like me to focus my note taking on? What type of notes will be most useful to you?	

Feedback process in simulated situations or live experiences

Step	Description	Sample prompts	Your prompts
Post-simulation or observation	a. Remind the learner of the feedback process.	a. Let's review our plan for this feedback session. What was the process we agreed to use? What is your role? What is mine? Based on the coaching session, I wonder if this process still makes sense to you.	
	b. Invite the learner to share reactions and feelings about the simulation or observation.	b. Based on what happened, what are your thoughts about this coaching experience both for you and the teacher?	
	c. Affirm elements of the learner's performance that meet or exceed the expected criteria.	c. Considering the expectations of coaches and your goals, what are some behaviors you feel were effective in this coaching session and how are you determining their effectiveness?	
	d. Identify elements that are borderline or did not meet expectations.	d. When considering those same expectations, what are some areas you want to continue to refine because you do not think they meet expectations? How do you know those areas are not meeting expectations?	
	e. Review the challenges from the presimulation conversation.	e. We talked about several challenges that might occur in this coaching session. Which if any occurred and how did you address them? What else occurred that you didn't anticipate?	
	f. Encourage dialogue to clarify future goals; maintain and/or extend the learner's performance; explore the learner's understanding of her performance; and develop strategies for improving performance.	f. Let's consider some next steps. Based on this coaching session, how will your professional growth goal change? What do you consider to be your strengths now and your areas for continued growth? What is your plan going forward from here to refine your practice as a coach? How can I support you in doing that? What other resources or support do you want to accomplish your plan?	
	g. Provide opportunities for continued practice.	g. How can I support you in doing that? What other resources or support do you want to accomplish your plan?	

Source: Adapted from Feedback in clinical procedural skills simulations by D. Nestel, F. Bello, and R. Kneebone.
In E. Molloy and D. Boud (Eds.) *Feedback in higher and professional educaton: Understanding and doing it well,* 2013, p. 145.

Feedback Evidence

7

IN THIS CHAPTER

Readers examine a discussion about the distinction between data and evidence. Readers will:

- Review the importance of reliability and validity on the quality of data that comprise sets of evidence.
- Engage with a case study that demonstrates how to consider type, source, and amount of data for data collection that results in strong data.
- Reflect on experiences with data collection to build evidence on which to make an assessment or a decision.
- Use the tool to build a data plan to use in a feedback process.

Data and evidence support and enhance the feedback process. The type and amount of evidence influence the quality of information utilized in constructing and deconstructing knowledge. The Data standard for professional learning (see sidebar) stresses the importance of having multiple types and sources of data to support decision making about professional learning. In any circumstance that requires data, data quality matters. This chapter explores the difference between data and evidence and how they are used in the feedback process.

Data vs. evidence

Scientists, social scientists, and philosophers have debated the distinction between data and evidence. The distinction is neither clearly known nor widely accepted among practitioners. There are, among scholars, some generally held distinctions grounded in the

Data Standard

Professional learning that increases educator effectiveness and results for all students uses a variety of sources and types of student, educator, and system data to plan, assess, and evaluate professional learning.

Standards for Professional Learning, 2011. http://learningforward.org/standards/data#.

fields of philosophy, research, and evidence-based medicine (Clarke, 2013). In an address at a meeting of the National Research Council (2001), Robert Mislevy, quoted in a report on the meeting states, "Datum becomes evidence in some analytic problem when its relevance to conjectures being considered is established." The report continues,

> Any piece of evidence, he argued, is almost always "incomplete, inconclusive, and amenable to multiple explanations." He also said that

using evidence to make inferences — explanations, conclusions, or predictions based on what we know and observe — is always done in the presence of uncertainty. (p. 11)

In the feedback process, it is helpful to understand in general the distinction between data and evidence. The feedback process builds on data — discrete information about individual circumstances, incidents, or practices — and through a process of reasoning turns the data into evidence to support the formation of new knowledge.

A datum is like an individual snapshot or single memento from a trip. When combined collectively with all of the snapshots and keepsakes from the same trip, they present a fuller picture of the experience. Imagine there is a single picture of people in front of Notre Dame Cathedral. It provides a glimpse of one moment in the trip. When it is combined with other photos of the same people and other landmarks in Paris such as the Eiffel Tower at night, sidewalk cafes, the Louvre, and the Arc de Triumph and souvenirs, they portray multiple images of the trip, the sights visited, and the experiences the travelers had. Each individual item is one part of the fall vacation to France, one point of data, or a datum. The collection of images and souvenirs together comprise the evidence. Through multiple experiences a traveler analyzes the evidence and compares and contrasts life in France and the US. The traveler uses the analyzed evidence to construct knowledge about the history and culture of France, daily living in France, the French people, and their customs. When the learner examines her evidence, she is able to deconstruct what she knows about France and the US and identify which aspects of French culture and life would not be appropriate in other countries.

Data are discrete bits of information that become evidence through a process of analysis and interpretation. Data translated into evidence serve as the foundation upon which learners construct knowledge. For example, a supervisor may have specific data about the number of times an employee interrupts a co-worker during a meeting (Datum 1: 6 times in a 30-minute period). The employee's supervisor may also have drawn on other data such as a perception of the co-worker's participation in meetings (Datum 2: Multiple substantive contributions in 12 of 12 meetings before the interruptions) and additional data about the co-worker's participation after the interruptions (Datum 3: 0 times in each of 3 recent meetings). The supervisor considers the new data with past data to construct a body of evidence, which he analyzes to form an inference about the relationship between the employee's behavior and the co-worker's response; namely, the co-worker stopped contributing to the discussion. The supervisor constructed evidence — action and response — from the data, which included frequency of behaviors and patterns of occurrences of the co-worker's behavior in response to the interruptions. He then used that evidence to construct knowledge about the employee's behavior and its impact on the co-worker (see Figure 7.1 on p. 81).

To some, making the distinction between data and evidence may seem unnecessary. Yet, the distinction is helpful, especially at the higher levels of the feedback process in the development of a learner's ability to analyze her own practice, construct, and then deconstruct knowledge from it. First, understanding the distinction is one way for a learner to develop capacity to identify and collect data from the learning object. He then pools the data to formulate evidence, which he analyzes to inform

Figure 7.1: **Data to Evidence for the Feedback Process**

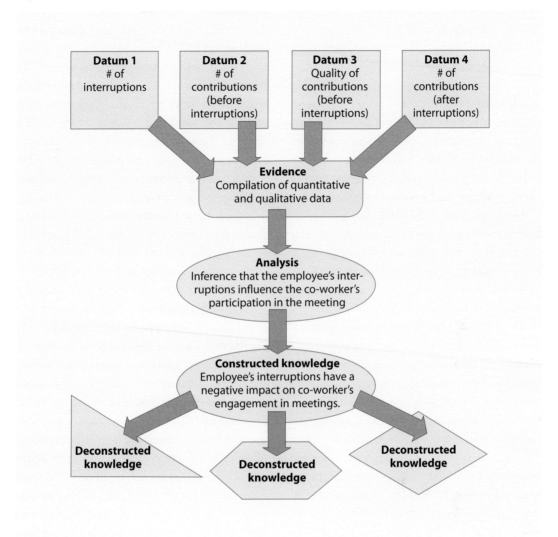

the construction of new knowledge during the feedback process. Second, making the process explicit, public, and transparent teaches learners how to turn data into evidence and how to analyze that evidence, and eventually, to use it to construct and deconstruct knowledge. Finally, applying data and evidence signifies a learner's commitment to intellectual rigor and deep learning, and increases the integrity of the feedback process.

Types of data

There are two types of data, qualitative and quantitative. Qualitative data are expressed in words, text, or video, image, or sound recordings. Qualitative data include perceptions, feelings, or observations described in words or text, work products, video recordings, sound recordings, or photographs. Quantitative data are expressed numerically and have the capacity to be manipulated, although not all quantitative data are expressed in formats that can be manipulated if they are continuous and have a defined scale. Quantitative data might also include perceptions, feelings, and observations described as numerical values such as responses on a survey using a Likert scale or on a rubric that describes levels of practice. Tools such as these translate perceptions, opinions, or practice to a number that conveys a quality or frequency. One example is assigning a score of 3 to indicate that a particular practice met a specific level of quality during an observation. Another example of quantitative data is the number of incidents, such as using a score of 3 to indicate that a particular practice occurred between five and eight times within a particular observation.

For the purpose of the feedback process, both types of data have a role. Qualitative data provide an opportunity to describe specific practices that occur and the circumstances in which they occur while quantitative data provide information on the frequency or rating of practices that occur. For example, when gathering data on public speaking, a learning partner notes that the learner uses the phrase *umm* 12 times in a three-minute period. Yet, with qualitative data, the learner is able to determine that the use of *umm* is preceded by a shift in the position of eye contact with the audience. Each time the learner glances in a different direction to maintain eye contact with the audience, she says *umm*. The frequency of the incidents of *umm* is important to note, yet the more important learning for the learner is likely to occur as she examines what might be occurring metacognitively as she shifts her focus and how that shift is associated with the verbal expression.

Combining qualitative and quantitative data can provide a broader pool of data that leads to a richer body of evidence. A learner benefits from both quantitative and qualitative data within the feedback process. Quantitative data provide a snapshot of practice, yet may not provide sufficient information to help the learner understand or explain her practice or what might influence it. Increased consciousness about one's metacognitive processes emerges from analysis of both quantitative and qualitative data and provides insights to help a learner understand, unpack, and explain her practice and use the data to develop evidence and eventually knowledge to inform future practices.

Reliability vs. validity

Other key concepts to consider in the types of data are reliability and validity, which are criteria of effective assessment and evaluation. These concepts apply to data used in the feedback process as well. Reliability is the degree to which data are consistent and stable across multiple settings. For example, a learning partner collects data about learner's ability to listen effectively, i.e. the learner uses paraphrasing across multiple, distinct situations. Evidence from the compiled data facilitates analysis and may lead to an inference about the factors that influence the pattern of practice and eventually to knowledge about how the pattern of practice influences and is influenced by the learner, others, and the context. If there are significant inconsistencies in data across multiple situations, the collected evidence would be weaker, and any inference or judgment about a learner's ability to listen effectively based on the evidence would be less reliable. A supportable conclusion, in that case, might be that the practice is inconsistent and varies across situations.

Too often in the feedback process, an assumption of reliability is made when there are insufficient data to warrant such an assumption. When only a single source or type of data is available, the reliability and validity of the data are less certain. Other challenges related to reliability of data occur when evidence is not solidly grounded in data and when other factors such as the learner's self-perception, relationship to a learner partner, the circumstances within which the feedback process occurs, or others are influencing decisions about which data to collect and combine to form a body of evidence.

Reliability of data is necessary but insufficient in the feedback process. Reliability must be combined with validity of data to increase levels of accuracy and certainty. Validity is the accuracy in measurement. In other words, it is the degree to which any data are accurate indicators of what they purport to represent. When a school district wants to engage coaches in the feedback process, the professional development director deploys a survey to collect teachers' perceptions several times within a school year about the usefulness of the coaching support they received. The director realizes that sometimes people will equate enjoyment with usefulness. She knows it is critical that the items on the survey accurately measure the specific construct they intend to study, namely usefulness. If the survey questions are misaligned with the construct, or are confusing, the data that emerge from the survey responses may be invalid. Defining or operationalizing the constructs and writing survey questions that align with those constructs are tasks that must be completed with careful thought. Otherwise, they could confound the validity of a measurement tool and have a negative effect on the quality of the data collected.

Here is another example of the importance of validity in data: A teacher sets a goal to increase higher-order thinking in student-to-student interaction during classroom discussions as part of social studies lessons. He asks a colleague to assist by collecting data about student interactions. They decide to use a sociogram, based on a seating chart, to record the direction of interaction among students in small- and large-group discussions over a three-day period. At the end three days, the teacher studies the sociograms, observes patterns of interactions among students, and notices increased frequency of student-to-student interactions over the three days.

The sociograms serve as valid data for the number and directionality of interactions among students, yet they are not valid sources of data for measuring whether those interactions represent higher-order thinking since they provide no information about the types of interactions. To increase the validity of the data, the observer would need to code student interaction using a coding system that distinguishes higher-order thinking interactions from those that are not, record the specific interactions, or record within the sociogram only interactions that meet the criteria of being higher-order thinking interactions. Trustworthiness of data is a significant factor to consider both prior to collecting data and in combining data to form a body of evidence.

Data sources

Data come from both human and inanimate sources. Human sources are people who are likely to have information relative to the practice. Inanimate sources are artifacts that provide information. Table 7.1 on page 84 lists both types of sources.

Multiple sources of data abound, yet not all sources are reliable and valid for every situation. For example, a school district's leaders administer a survey to staff about the efficiency of district operations. The survey asks about specific conditions within a school and the relationship

Table 7.1: **Data Sources Common in Education**

Human data sources	Inanimate data sources

• Learner
 	
• Supervisor
 	
• Administrators
 	
• Colleagues/peers
 	
• Mentors
 	
• Coaches
 	
• Clients (such as students, parents, community members)
 	
• Program managers, facilitators, leaders, faculty, etc.
 	
• Participants/members of a program, community of learners, network, etc.
 	
• External partners (e.g. institutes of higher education faculty, regional, state, or provincial agency staff, vendors, etc.)
	• Work products
	  - Notes
	  - Logs
	  - Minutes
	  - Plans
	  - Reports
	  - Assessments
	  - Lesson and unit plans
	  - Communications
	  - Participation records
	  - Observation notes and reports
	  - Performance evaluations
	• Client (student, faculty, staff, program participant, etc.) work products
	• Formative or summative assessment data
	• Description of practice
	• Notes from observations of practice

among staff and school administrators, staff engagement in decisions related to instruction, curriculum, and working conditions, and staff satisfaction with their role. It also asks for suggestions about district operations. Some school staff might have information about district operations; other may not. Equating school conditions with district ones is misleading and may not accurately portray district operations. The survey may be less valid as a measure of district operations and more valid as a measure of school operations.

The quality, source, and amount of data influence the results of the feedback process. **Strong** data are those that come from multiple sources, are of different types, and are both reliable and valid. When data are **weak** — there is a small amount of data from a single source or only one type of data — and are insufficiently reliable and valid, the result of the feedback process may also be weak. When high-stakes decisions are being made within or as a result of the feedback process, it is crucial to use data that are both reliable and valid. For lower-stakes decisions the rigor of data quality in the feedback process may be relaxed. Learners should have clear understanding about the types and sources of data that are being collected and used within the feedback process. Whenever reasonable when external learning partners are involved in the feedback process, learners should be actively involved in and mutually agree to the types and amount of data to be collected and the format in which it will be collected. The Case Study of Strong Data on pages 85 shows how a teacher leader goes about planning for and collecting data and evidence to inform his progress on meeting a learning goal. After studying the case study, readers may use Tool 7.1: *Data plan template* for their own data collection and analysis.

Case Study of Strong Data

A teacher leader, new in his role, has established a goal to acquire and practice facilitation skills that will increase collaboration among members of the team he leads. The success of his goal is dependent on team members' engagement and the shared results they achieve for students. Specifically, he wants members to

- perceive that they are valued members of the team;
- be active contributors at each meeting;
- assume responsibility to shape the team's agenda;
- be accountable for the team's student results;
- have strategies to accomplish their goals efficiently and effectively;
- be able to be honest with one another; and
- engage in conflict productively.

At the end of the year, he wants team members to demonstrate that their student achievement is positively influenced by the team's productive and efficient collaboration. He meets with the team weekly and has multiple opportunities to practice a variety of facilitation skills.

Over a three-month period he collects different types of qualitative and quantitative data for use in both self-initiated and supervisor-driven feedback processes (see table that follows). He meets monthly with his supervisor, reflects after each meeting independently using data, and asks members of the team to engage with him in a feedback process to analyze his facilitation skills. At the end of the first quarter of the school year, he will have a supervisory meeting with his principal about his progress as a teacher leader. The list below shows the various ways he collects data and demonstrates that he has strong data to support the evidence he will provide to his supervisor about how well he achieves his goal.

Month	Data source	Specific data collection method and source	Data type*
September	Teacher leader	Work products: Agenda and minutes	ABC
	Team members	Team member perceptions: Team effectiveness survey	ABC or 123
	Team members	Team member perceptions: Sense of belonging and responsibility survey	ABC or 123
	Team members	Team member behaviors: Contribution counts and attendance	123
	Colleague	Observation notes: Ratio of facilitator-member interaction	ABC
October	Supervisor	Observation notes: Facilitator behaviors	ABC
	Team members	Team member perceptions: Discussion notes	ABC
	Team members	Team member perceptions: Team effectiveness survey	123
	Students	Assessment data: Student common assessment scores and work products	123 and ABC
November	Teacher leader	Work products: Team action plan; team's quarterly progress report; critical events analysis form	ABC
	Team members	Team member perceptions: Team strengths and weaknesses; recommendations for team leader	ABC
	Colleagues	Observation notes: Teacher leader questions and listening behaviors	ABC
	Supervisor	Observation notes: Teacher-leader performance rubric scores	123

* ABC = Qualitative
123 = Quantitative

Conclusion

Data are a critical component of the feedback process. Both qualitative and quantitative data are appropriate in the feedback process if the data are from multiple sources and are valid and reliable. Data become evidence to support judgments, analyses, assessments, and construction and deconstruction of knowledge. Evidence illuminates and explains practice, and informs decisions about next actions for refining practice. Reliable and valid data from multiple sources and of different types strengthen the feedback process. When high-stakes decisions are made within and as a result of the feedback process, it is particularly important to ensure that high-quality data are collected and used.

The distinction between data and evidence is not only nice to know; it also increases the veracity of the evidence. Turning data into evidence strengthens and solidifies the support for analysis and construction. When inferences are drawn from one or two data points, they are less valid and reliable. Data from multiple sources and in different forms create more convincing and trustworthy evidence. When the evidence is stronger, learners are able to construct more useful and specific knowledge.

Reflections

1. Give at least two examples of data and evidence from a recent situation to demonstrate your understanding of the distinction between data and evidence.

2. Reliability and validity are two attributes of high-quality data. For one of the situations you identified above cite an example of high and low reliability and high and low validity data sources or types.

3. In the context in which you work, which form of data, qualitative or quantitative, is more commonly used? What are possible factors contributing to this usage?

4. Using the model of the teacher leader's plan to collect data to build a body of evidence for his quarterly meeting with his supervisor, create a list of multiple types and sources of data for one of your professional growth goals.

5. Consider the feedback situations in which you are engaged on a routine basis. Assess the reliability and validity of the data used in those situations. Explain your assessment and recommend what might be done to strengthen the reliability and validity of the data if they fall short of meeting the standard of high quality.

References

Clarke, B. (2013, July 22). What's the difference between evidence and data? UCL Department of Science and Technology Studies. Available at http://www.ucl.ac.uk/sts/ staff/clarke/data-evidence_distinction.

Towne, L., Shavelson, R., Feuer, M. (Eds). (2001). *Science, evidence, and inference in education: Report of a workshop.* Committee on Scientific Principles in Education Research. Division of Behavioral and Social Sciences and Education, National Research Council. Washington, DC: National Academy Press. Available at http://www.nap.edu/catalog/10121.html.

TOOL 7.1

Data plan template

Use this template to plan data collection for use in the feedback process.

Time period	Data source	Specific data collection method and source	Data type ABC = Qualitative 123 = Quantitative

System
Feedback

8

IN THIS CHAPTER Readers consider what the idea of systems thinking means for their own schools and districts. Readers will:

- Contrast *open* and *closed* systems and the implications for local systems.
- Understand how to discover and address *reinforcing* and *balancing* feedback processes.
- Reflect on how systems thinking may apply to the analysis and improvement of their own classrooms, schools, or districts.
- Use the tool to analyze the usefulness of current feedback systems.

The feedback process improves performance of individuals, teams, and systems. Previous chapters discussed the use of the feedback process with individuals and teams. This chapter examines how systems use the feedback process to strengthen results, efficiency, and effectiveness.

A system is a collection of interconnected components whose actions influence the actions of other components and the system as a whole. Two types of systems exist: closed and open. To closed systems, the external environment is static and predictable; thus, it has no influence on the system. Therefore, closed systems are sealed off from the outside world and explain the performance of individuals, teams, and the system itself relative to the internal system operations and dynamics within the system. To change closed systems, leaders change internal processes, components, and their interactions.

Open systems interact with external variables and, as a result, are influenced by the external environment. Local and federal policies, economy, globalization, resource availability, technological advances, demographic factors, and social conditions are some external influences that influence systems. Open systems change by adjusting the way they interact with external variables.

Some leaders consider education to be an open system because so many external factors influence the operations of schools. Those wanting to change open systems understand that deep change results from altering both internal as well as external factors. Others treat education as a closed system because some educators are hesitant to claim responsibility for or influence on external factors. When schools and school systems are treated as closed systems those striving to make change look only inside the system to explain problems or challenges that occur and to find appropriate solutions. Whether leaders treat the systems in which they work as open or closed, they depend on the feedback process to understand their current practice, determine appropriate actions to strengthen it, and construct knowledge to apply to subsequent practice. Just as with learning-focused feedback processes that strengthen the practice of individuals and teams, systems use the learning-focused feedback process to construct knowledge from high-quality data converted to evidence, strong analytic reasoning, and clear processes.

Systems-thinking approach

For feedback processes to work well within systems, leaders and members use data and evidence that focus on helping systems construct "learning to recognize types of 'structures' that reoccur again and again" (Senge, 1990, p. 73). These structures have either a positive or negative effect on the system's effectiveness and performance and explain the types of inter-relationships and patterns that may promote or block change, growth, or progress.

Peter Senge (1990) proposed that the feedback process in systems is the reciprocal interaction of causes and effects. He stresses that nothing is ever influenced in one direction. He also emphasizes that how causes and effects are described either open or limit deeper understanding and potential to change. In Senge's view, the ability to engage in feedback processes within organizations is distinguished by increasing understanding of the multidirectionality of influences and the way they interact to affect cause-and-effect relationships. Any individual within a system is therefore a part of the system and is naturally both an influence on and influenced by the system.

His work inspired other thought leaders who posit that some changes are adaptive and some are technical. Technical changes are those that can be addressed with known

procedures, strategies, or tactics and may work within closed systems. Adaptive changes require a new approach, the construction of ways to view and address the changes that are not yet known. Such changes always require an open system perspective that considers the internal and external factors influencing the system. In the realm of feedback, adaptive changes require higher-order feedback, and technical changes may suffice with lower-order feedback (Heifetz, Grashow, & Lensky, 2009).

Among Senge's (1990) major contributions to the world of systems thinking is his view of how feedback processes provide the language needed to describe system archetypes. He recommends that organizations discover their embedded *reinforcing* and *balancing* feedback forces through the application of the feedback process. Both, he notes, provide information to the system, hence their role as feedback processes that have the potential to effect progress and growth (see Figure 8.1 on p. 91).

When school leaders struggle to address low student achievement, they often take measures to increase instructional time by decreasing recess and expanding instructional time for tested subjects such as reading and math. Yet more of the same kind of instruction does not necessarily increase students' learning. Focusing on reading and math in isolation of other disciplines such as social studies, science, humanities, or fine arts reduces students' opportunities to apply learning in authentic ways. Without feedback systems that allow school leaders to study the incremental and long-term impacts of their decisions overall, student learning may not increase. A responsible feedback system would highlight the dynamics that occur when multiple systems interact such as the curriculum, instruction, teachers' and principals' professional learning, district resources and support to schools and classrooms, and interventions

Figure 8.1: **Growing and Limiting Systems Approach**

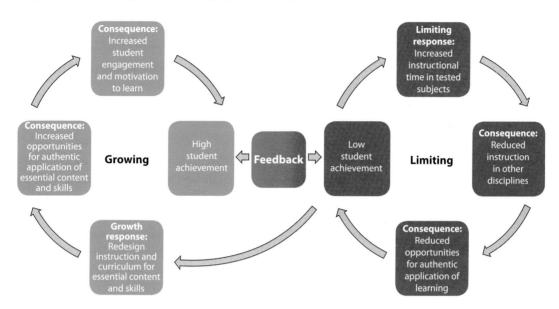

and supports available to students and families within the school and community.

A feedback system would also help decision makers see that the simple solution of increasing time in instruction without changing other related areas will lead to the same results. Consequently, leaders' fundamental assumptions may require adjustment and their typical technical changes may need to give way to adaptive ones. Low student achievement, for example, may well require increasing instruction time. It may mean that instruction must focus on high-priority knowledge and skills applied in multiple real-life performance tasks to increase engagement and deepen understanding. It may also mean that instruction, curriculum, and assessment will need to change so that students have meaningful opportunities to use their learning. Changing how educators design and facilitate instruction, how frequently they collect and use data about student learning to adapt instruction, and how they apply interventions for students needing

remediation or enrichment are more likely to increase the relevance and retention of the learning than simply adjusting instructional time. Likewise, when community and family support for education increases and students' physical, social, and emotional well-being improves, student academic success is likely to be positively affected. Systems feedback lets leaders look beyond simplistic technical actions to enact adaptive actions that leverage other related systems for a more powerful influence on the results.

Reinforcing and balancing processes in systems

Systems contain reinforcing and balancing processes designed to provide continuous feedback. Reinforcing processes amplify growth or decline. These small, often unnoticeable actions multiply and grow, sometimes unintentionally, until they eventually affect the outcomes. Occasionally, the factors influencing changes or the changes those factors produce are unknown to system managers until the effects are significant. Most reinforcing processes are positive in nature, and because they contribute to positive results, they are more difficult to discern. When an organization, for example, funds an employee-recognition program based on employee attendance, the organization finds that attendance at work increases. Initially the increased attendance has a small increase on productivity. Over time, increased attendance has a greater effect on productivity. As success of the attendance recognition program increases, the organization provides recognition programs for other workplace behaviors. Company leaders perceive the cause-effect relationship between the recognition programs and increased productivity, yet may be unable to discern how related factors, such as increased morale, commitment, and sense of being valued, may influence reduced absenteeism and increased productivity. Other recognition programs may be less successful because leaders may only see the simple cause-effect relationship without identifying other mediating factors that potentially influence results of the attendance recognition programs.

Reinforcing processes also influence decline in the same way they influence continued growth. A principal favors an impending change and values supportive, positive public comments about it. She prefers to receive negative comments in private. That preference influences her actions during meetings in regard to who is allowed or invited to speak. The colleagues who are unsupportive of the initiative feel oppressed; consequently, that feeling fuels further dissent about the initiative's value. When the principal is able to engage in the feedback process, and analyze how her behavior affects support for and opposition to the initiative, she may discover the relationship between her actions and the undesirable effect.

Reinforcing processes usually occur simultaneously with balancing processes. Balancing processes set limits defined by an implicit or explicit goal. As the goal is achieved, the system shuts down, thereby limiting growth beyond the goal. Senge (1990) explains:

> A biologist would say that these processes are the mechanism by which our body maintains homeostasis — its ability to maintain conditions for survival in changing environment. Balancing feedback prompts us to eat when we need food, and to sleep when we need rest, or… to put on a sweater when we are cold. (pp. 84–85)

He cites an example of an organization that reduces its workforce to address a downturn in its economic conditions. As a result of the reduction in employees, those remaining must assume greater responsibility, and work harder and longer hours to accomplish an unchanged output. The organization, to maintain its current output, expends additional funds to hire consultants and pay employees overtime. These expenditures have a negative effect on the intended budget savings. Through the feedback process, systems have opportunities to examine evidence to determine the effect of practices to ensure they are producing the intended rather than unintended results.

The feedback process is essential to support system change. Because systems tend to maintain their status quo, education decision makers need to be able to examine deeply the reinforcing and balancing processes within the system to determine their impact on the overall effectiveness of the system. Only then can they determine how the processes may inadvertently be serving as reinforcing or balancing processes that are positively or negatively affecting the system's success. Knowing what influences change positively or negatively becomes knowledge educators can use to shape future practice and achieve desirable outcomes. When decision makers recognize the positive influences, they can replicate them to generate additional positive outcomes. Likewise, when decision makers know the negative influences, they can avoid or change those influences. For systems to develop and benefit from feedback processes, systems leaders must gather data, form bodies of evidence, examine the evidence from multiple perspectives with a ruthless, no-holds-barred approach that allows them to identify potentially negative reinforcing processes and balancing processes that interfere with success. To help deepen understanding and consider multiple cause-and-effect relationships, system leaders engage multiple stakeholders in the system feedback processes.

Feedback sources for systems

As in the feedback process for individuals and teams, data come from both human and inanimate sources. For systems feedback processes in education, some examples of data sources include surveys of student, staff, parent, community, institutes of higher education, and suppliers; formative and summative student performance data; efficiency measures, financial reports, external audits, or program reviews. Reports, plans, policies, guidance documents, administrative procedures, handbooks, communications, and practice audits are other data sources. Common tools for accessing data about systems include benchmarking, auditing, customer surveys, employee satisfaction surveys, 360° surveys, and artifact analysis. Again, just as they do in feedback processes for individuals or teams, the types and sources of data matter as do their reliability and validity.

When planning to engage in feedback processes to inform systems, education decision makers benefit from systemwide analysis based on a broad base of evidence rather than a limited examination of individual components or subsystems. For example, a superintendent's cabinet examining the effectiveness of the school district's human capital management system, a subsystem within the larger education system, must look at its component parts — hiring, placement, onboarding, continuous professional learning, support systems, and performance appraisal. They must also come to an understanding about how this single subsystem interacts with other subsystems that make up the larger education system. Without taking a broader systems view, the district decision makers have limited opportunity to construct knowledge about the entire human capital management system. Furthermore, taking a narrow view restricts a leader's ability to understand how the human capital management system contributes to the success or failure of other subsystems and the system as a whole.

To engage in a systemwide feedback process, it is essential to:

- Collect data on multiple related components of a subsystem and the other subsystems it interacts with to illuminate cause-effect relationships. When examining data on student achievement, for instance, it is also important to examine the alignment of curriculum and the assessments or tests, content standards, instructional resources, professional learning, human capital management, and family factors that may influence student academic success;

- Identify and map cause-effect relationships among the components of a subsystem and its related subsytems using flowcharts, maps, modeling, or other means to show the interactions among the subsystems and their components. It is also advantageous to apply guidance from performance management systems such as Balanced Scorecard (Kaplan & Norton, 1996). Balanced Scorecard links four distinct areas that influence organization performance. Those areas include translating the vision into strategic actions; communicating and linking; business planning; and feedback and learning (1996). Other similar strategic performance management systems also exist. In schools, some subsystems include human capital management; curriculum and instruction; facilities and materials management; data and assessment; policy and governance;

- Examine immediate and distant relationships among subsystems within and outside the school system to identify potential leverage for positively changing results;
- Construct findings, conclusions, or generalizations supported by the data analyses;
- Plan, implement, monitor, and assess deliberate strategies and tactics to redesign components or subsystems to increase efficiency, effectiveness, and results; and
- Implement processes to generate continuous data to use in making ongoing decisions to adjust and refine components within subsystems or whole subsystems.

Conclusion

Because of their complexity, systems face particular challenges with the introduction of new initiatives. By their very nature of being contained within a system, initiatives are affected by every component part or whole subsystem and affect those components and subsystem. When any one part of a system changes within a larger, interconnected system, other parts react. The effects may occur immediately and may be visible or they may be delayed and more difficult to discern. The challenge is to determine the relationships among the components or subsystems to be able to address the reinforcing and balancing process that may limit growth.

When planned or unintentional reinforcing and balancing processes are in place, it is more difficult to determine which cause-effect linkages occur and which have the greatest impact on results. As a result, feedback processes are essential to allow leaders to identify, track, manage, and adjust the dynamic interplay among component parts or subsystems within a larger system (see Tool 8.1: *Feedback within systems*). Without feedback processes to disrupt limiting processes that interfere with change, systems may self-correct and reinforce the status quo.

Reflections

1. Consider the distinctions between a closed and open system. Which do you consider education in general? A district? A school? Explain your thinking.

2. Identify a recent change initiative that you have been associated with. Was the approach to the change technical or adaptive? How successful was the change? Consider how the approach to the change influenced the results.

3. How does your system use the feedback process to improve its overall results? Cite specific examples.

4. What are some examples of reinforcing and balancing feedback processes that influence your system?

5. What types of data are available to guide system change? How are those data used?

References

Heifetz, R., Grashow, A., & Lensky, M. (2009). *The practice of adaptive leadership: Tools and tactics for changing your organization and the world.* Boston, MA: Harvard Business Press.

Kaplan, R. & Norton, D. (1996). Using the Balanced Scorecard as a strategic management system. *Harvard Business Review, 74*(1), 75–85.

Senge, P. (1990). *The fifth discipline: The art & practice of the learning organization.* New York, NY: Doubleday/Currency.

Feedback within systems

Use this tool to analyze the current feedback systems associated with existing systems and determine changes needed to improve the usefulness of the feedback system. The table includes a sample for a feedback system on professional learning.

Systems	Current feedback	Overall usefulness of current feedback (use rubric below)	Changes needed
Sample: Professional learning	Satisfaction surveys given at the end of programs, courses, workshops, etc.		Accessibility of data by all stakeholders; more sources; more types of data; data about impact of system on educators and students; increased use of data.

Feedback within systems

Score	1 (low)	2	3	4	5 (high)
Accessibility	A feedback system is available.	A feedback system is accessible.	A feedback system is easily accessible by leaders.	A feedback system is easily accessible by key stakeholders.	A feedback system is easily accessible by all stakeholders.
Frequency of access	Data from the feedback system are accessed annually.	Data from the feedback system are accessed semi-annually.	Data from the feedback system are accessed quarterly.	Data from the feedback system are accessed monthly.	Data from the feedback system are accessed weekly.
Flexibility	The feedback system cannot be queried.	The feedback system provides static data.	The feedback system can be queried using pre-established search criteria.	The feedback system can be queried using limited user-generated search criteria.	The feedback system can be queried using extensive user-generated and relevant search criteria.
Types of data	The feedback system offers one type of data.	The feedback system offers one type of qualitative data and one type of quantitative data.	The feedback system offers at least two types of qualitative and quantitative data.	The feedback system provides three types of qualitative and qualitative data.	The feedback system provides four or more types of qualitative and quantitative data.
Sources of data	The feedback system provides data from one source.	The feedback system provides data from two sources.	The feedback system provides data from three sources.	The feedback system provides data from four sources.	The feedback system provides data from five or more sources.
Content of feedback system	The feedback system offers limited data about the system's efficiency or effectiveness.	The feedback system offers limited data about the system's efficiency or effectiveness.	The feedback system offers valid or reliable data that that lead to evidence about the efficiency and effectiveness of the system.	The feedback system offers valid and reliable data that lead to evidence about the efficiency and effectiveness of the system.	The feedback system offers valid and reliable data that lead to evidence about the efficiency, effectiveness, and the impact of the system.

Feedback within systems

Score	1 (low)	2	3	4	5 (high)
Frequency of use of data	Data from the feedback system are reviewed annually to make adjustments in the system.	Data from the feedback system are reviewed semi-annually to make adjustments in the system.	Data from the feedback system are used quarterly to make adjustments in the system.	Data from the feedback system are used monthly to make adjustments in the system.	Data from the feedback system are used weekly to make adjustments in the system.
Results of the feedback system	The feedback system contributes to annual improvements.	The feedback system contributes to semi-annual improvements.	The feedback system contributes to quarterly improvements.	The feedback system contributes to monthly improvements.	The feedback system contributes to weekly improvements.
Evaluation of feedback system	The feedback system is not reviewed or evaluated.	The feedback system is reviewed periodically.	The feedback system is evaluated annually.	The feedback system is evaluated quarterly.	The feedback system is continuously evaluated.
Improvement in feedback system	Improvements are not made in the feedback system.	The feedback system is improved annually.	The feedback system is improved semi-annually based on evaluation data.	The feedback system is improved quarterly based on evaluation data.	The feedback system is improved continuously based on evaluation data.

Future of Learning-focused Feedback

9

IN THIS CHAPTER Readers consider the implications of policy and practice to develop individual and system capacity and culture for learning-focused feedback. Readers will:

- Consider the tensions between the feedback process and existing policies for performance appraisal.
- Apply the policy development cycle to draft policies addressing the feedback process.
- Reflect on the state of district policy, expertise, and capacity to use the feedback process.
- Use the tool to begin examination of existing policies governing feedback process.

Making the feedback process a reality for professionals will require systemic action at both the policy and practice levels. This chapter outlines some of the changes needed to realize this new view of feedback in professional learning.

Policy changes

Policies related to preparation, ongoing support, induction, and supervision specify the purpose, context, and structure of the feedback educators receive. These policies tend to formalize feedback as one-way, externally generated information primarily from a professor, mentor, coach, supervisor, or another knowledgeable other. To embed the feedback process into routine practice, policies regarding analysis of, assessment of, reflection on, and evaluation of professional practice must be grounded in a set of principles that clearly delineate the purpose, direction, and responsibility in the feedback process.

The clauses of the *Agenda for Change* (Osney Grange Group, 2009) serve as an example of the assumptions that underlie policies supporting feedback as a process for promoting growth. The *Agenda for Change*, a proposal generated by international experts on assessment and feedback in higher education, resulted from a discussion among researchers, writers, and practitioners about the theory and practice of feedback.

The Osney Grange Group proposes the following clauses within its *Agenda for Change*:

Clause 1: It needs to be acknowledged that high level and complex learning are best developed when feedback is seen as a relational process that takes place over time, is dialogic, and is integral to learning and teaching.

Clause 2: There needs to be recognition that valuable and effective

www.learningforward.org

feedback can come from varied sources, but if [adult] students do not learn to evaluate their own work they will remain completely dependent upon others. The abilities to complete self- and peer review are essential graduate attributes.

Clause 3: To facilitate and reinforce these changes there must be a fundamental review of policy and practice to move the focus to feedback as a process rather than a product. Catalysts for change would include revision of resourcing models, quality assurance processes and course structures, together with development of staff and student pedagogic literacies.

Clause 4: Widespread reconceptualisation of the role and purpose of feedback is only possible when stakeholders at all levels in higher education take responsibility for bringing about integrated change. In support of this reconceptualisation, use must be made of robust, research-informed guiding principles, and supporting materials.

Clause 5: *The Agenda for Change* calls on stakeholders to take steps towards bringing about necessary changes in policy and practice. (para. 3)

Policies that position feedback for professionals as a core component of the learning process whether in a supervisory, higher education, or professional learning function, address the following key principles:

- Feedback is a process rather than product.
- Feedback is a necessary component of the learning process.

- The primary purpose of feedback is learning to strengthen practice and increase results.
- Feedback is continuous, not occasional.
- Self-generated feedback, within this policy framework, is desirable and respected as valid and reliable.
- All professionals are responsible for developing the capacity to engage in and facilitate the feedback process that includes complex analysis.
- Resources, including time and professional learning, are available so that educators can integrate feedback as a routine process that occurs continuously within learning and professional practice.
- All stakeholders have an active role in developing, communicating, understanding, and using explicit criteria for excellence in professional practice.

One tension point in policies about the feedback process is its placement within performance reviews. Performance evaluation is a formal, legal function through which decisions about future employment, promotions, or pay are made. The feedback process may be applicable if the performance appraisal system includes a learning-focused phase in which the feedback process is appropriate as a precursor or component of the evaluation process. Not all performance evaluation, however, has the goal of promoting learning. As a result, what is often called feedback within that process falls outside the definition of feedback as described within this book.

The feedback process, on the other hand, generates learning when it moves to the right side of the continuum into knowledge construction and deconstruction. For true learning to occur, as Anna Carroll (2014) notes, the learner and learning partner must be on the same side of the table. Carroll speaks both figuratively and literally to the relative positions of learners and partners, because learning partners must want to promote learning as much as learners seek it. In performance reviews, she says, the employee and manager are on opposite sides of the table. Supervisors are engaging in a function determined through a formal process with a purpose different from learning. Douglas Stone and Sheila Heen (2014) claim that a single performance management system can't effectively complete the full range of types of feedback, which they say are appreciation, coaching, and evaluation. Coaching, by their definition, is closest to the right side of the feedback types continuum. They acknowledge that there are two problems with mixing coaching and evaluation:

> First, on the receiving end, my attention will be drawn to the evaluation, which drowns out the coaching. If I think I have lost the bonus I already promised my family, I'm not going to hear your suggestions for how I can tweak my PowerPoint slides. The second concern is that, if I am going to be open to coaching, I need to feel safe. I need to know that admitting mistakes or areas of weakness isn't going to count against me in my job security or career advancement. I need absolute trust that being open in coaching conversations will not adversely affect my evaluation. (p. 299)

When the same learning partner engages with a learner in both processes, the role responsibilities and relationships differ greatly. This difference causes the two functions to be confused and the feedback process to remain at the evaluation level. Daniel Pink (2011) calls performance reviews "kabuki theater" in which people say what is expected of them in

predictable ways. Carroll acknowledges that, "Performance review does have a definite role to play, but as feedback it is slow" (p. 61). Carroll quotes Samuel Culbert (2008):

> You would think that the person in the best position to help somebody improve would be his or her boss. Yet thanks to the performance review, the boss is often the last person an employee would turn to. People don't want to pay a high price for acknowledging their need for improvement, which is exactly what they would do if they arm the boss with the kind of personal information he or she would need to help them "develop." (pp. 63–64)

In establishing policy about feedback processes, decision makers need to explore, consider, and determine if the primary source of feedback for employees within an organization comes from supervisors within the performance review process or if there are alternative opportunities and learning partners with whom a learner engages in the feedback process in frequent, informal, and low-risk situations. When learners have learning partners who are different from their evaluators or supervisors, they may be more able to use their full capacity as a learner, without fear or defensiveness, to engage fully in the feedback process for learning.

Policies and guidelines that support implementation of an effective feedback process include, at a minimum, the following components:

- **Definition:** What is our common understanding of feedback and the feedback process?
- **Purposes of the feedback process:** What are the defined purposes and non-purposes of the feedback process within our organization?

- **Responsibility:** Who is responsible for preparing learners and learning partners for high-quality practice in the feedback process? Who is responsible for ensuring that all learners have access to opportunities to engage in fair and equitable feedback processes?
- **Quality:** What are the criteria of effective feedback processes? How do we maintain high-quality feedback processes? How do we use the criteria to monitor, assess, evaluate, and adjust the application of and results of feedback processes?

To develop such policies, policymakers must convene stakeholders to generate their own deep understanding of feedback and to shape desired practice with feedback. To accomplish this work, policymakers and stakeholders work collaboratively through a multistep process. The first step is the study of research on feedback in professional and higher education settings. The second is analysis of data about existing feedback practices drawn directly from the learners' current experiences and from those who have traditionally been the givers of feedback. The third step is an examination of the organization's and learners' beliefs and assumptions about feedback to determine which will serve as the foundation for their new policy and practice and which are barriers to successful implementation. Next, is development of the vision for, definition, and purposes of effective feedback processes within the organization; all of these policy elements are based on the study of data about current practice, assumptions, and beliefs. Following this step is designing indicators of quality and quality control, implementation, and the supports needed to ensure equitable access to and sustained quality of feedback processes. Once the core components of the policy are complete,

the focus turns to developing and implementing deep implementation.

Practice changes

Policy changes do not necessarily lead to changes in practice; deliberate efforts to reform feedback practices must be designed and implemented. The primary levers of practice change include cultivating the capacity of learners and learning partners to apply the feedback process routinely in practice.

To accomplish such changes in practice means building culture for new feedback practices along with the capacity. With policies in place, education leaders will need to invest effort, persistence, and other resources into the preparation and support of learners, learning partners, and their supervisors. Thoughtful attention to the development of expertise demands that decision makers change the more traditional approaches to professional learning as well. As D. Royce Sadler (2013) notes:

[R]esearch into human learning shows that there is only so much a person typically learns purely from being told … . Teaching by telling is commonly dubbed as the transmission model of teaching. It portrays teachers as repositories of knowledge, the act of teaching being to dispense, communicate or "impart" knowledge for students to learn … .By itself, [telling] is inadequate for complex learning. Being able to use, apply, and adapt knowledge, or to use it to create new knowledge requires more than merely absorbing information and reproducing it on demand. Educational research over the past few decades has recognized the need for students to interact with information and skills, to make these their own, to incorporate them into their existing knowledge bases and structures, and to "construct" or build knowledge that will serve them as adaptable personal capital. This emphasis may be relatively recent, but the process itself is what humans have always done. What has changed is the perspective. (pp. 55–56)

The transformation in feedback practice emerges when learners and their partners embrace a new view of feedback, have the capacity to implement the practices, and receive supports needed for deep and routine implementation. Capacity requires three essential components: skillfulness, mindfulness, and openness. These three components are necessary for learners and their learning partners.

Skillfulness. Skillfulness includes developing the competencies to engage in the feedback process with integrity. This includes the ability to communicate with precision; analyze and critique one's own practice; seek and use data from multiple sources as evidence that leads to conclusions about the effects of one's practice on others; formulate supportable conclusions or generalizations and testable hypotheses, examine how alternative contexts might affect the new knowledge, access resources to identify and support future actions that result in refinement and growth over time; and implement and assess the effectiveness of the refined actions. For learning partners, in addition to the skills listed, it includes expertise in facilitating the feedback process or to witness it in supportive ways.

Mindfulness. In addition to skillfulness, the feedback process requires mindfulness. Mindfulness is awareness of self and one's impact on others and the environment. It is

as Ellen Langer (1989) describes, the ability to create new categories into which we organize information, experiences, or perceptions. It also includes openness to process new information that does not currently fit within one's existing schema. Lastly, as Langer describes, mindfulness is the recognition that multiple perspectives exist. *Psychology Today* (2014) defines mindfulness as "a state of active, open attention on the present. When you're mindful, you observe your thoughts and feelings from a distance, without judging them good or bad. Instead of letting your life pass you by, mindfulness means living in the moment and awakening to experience." It is a desire to cultivate a deep sense of one's assumptions and beliefs and how they weave together and become the mental model that drives thought, words, and actions.

Particularly challenging in the feedback process is the mindfulness of the learning partner and his shift from being the knowledgeable other to being the partner in learning. Jane Vella describes the temptation of some to overshadow adults as they engage in learning by persisting in displaying "my erudition and depth of knowledge and skillfulness" (p. 119) or to "show how much I know about the new theory or how facile I am in this skill" (p. 119). She states that rather than showing off, she is better able to facilitate others' learning when she intentionally "follow[s] their learning and thus lead[s] them into more learning" (p. 119).

Within a learner, mindfulness emerges from an internal motivation to cultivate honesty and humility in self-analysis and reflection and eliminate defensiveness, which limits truthfulness and rigor in self-analysis and reflection. With commitment, a learner persists in seeking and using multiple forms of evidence to shape and reshape his understanding of the effects of his practice on himself, others, and the context. For learning partners, mindfulness about their role in the feedback process is essential. At the highest levels, the learning partner witnesses the feedback process rather than directs it.

Openness. The third essential component of practice is openness to discovery. With openness the unexpected is possible. Most learners seek certainty in the learning process and, as a result, carefully shield themselves from the unexpected based on a fear that their self-concept will be shaken. Yet when learners are open and enter the process with both skillfulness and mindfulness, they are rewarded with new levels of understanding. In the feedback process learning partners are open to developing new discoveries about how feedback promotes learning, to understanding how they influence learning of others, and how the learning of others contributes to their own learning.

Learner practice, either alone or with learning partners, that supports feedback includes frequent opportunities to pause and respond to these prompts:

- I am aware that [observations based on evidence from multiple perspectives];
- Based on this awareness I wonder [critical analyses driven by inquiries about the data in relationship to criteria, goal, or standards];
- As a result of my analysis, I am expanding/reshaping/revamping my learning [knowledge, skills, practices, desires, or dispositions];
- I am more aware of the significance of [conclusions] because …; and
- As a result I will [future actions to apply learning, test conclusions, explore new hypotheses, etc.].

Conclusion

Policies and practice alone will do little to change current practices in developing and using feedback in a dialogic way to promote learning. Both are necessary to ensure equity in opportunity for learners and learning partners to learn how to apply the feedback processes and to make and sustain systemic support for continuous application of the learning-focused feedback process (see Tool 9.1: *Examining current practice and policies about feedback*). Policymakers and system leaders who want to embed a learning-focused feedback process will make concerted efforts to pair policy change with practice change. Only then, may they begin to realize the full potential of the effective feedback process as a core component in continuous learning that leads to positive changes in professional practice and student results.

Reflections

1. What are your organization's existing assumptions about feedback? What are your personal ones?

2. What are your organization's existing policies about feedback?

3. How do those policies influence practices? How closely do these policies align with the assumptions you identified in Question 1? How will the degree of alignment influence the organization's ability to alter its existing policies and practices on feedback?

4. How widespread is expertise in feedback within the organization? Where does it seem to be strongest and weakest? What evidence supports that?

5. What changes in policy and practice are most essential to create, implement, and sustain the desired vision of feedback?

References

Carroll, A. (2014). *The feedback imperative: How to give everyday feedback to speed up your team's success.* Austin, TX: River Grove Books.

Culbert, S. (2008, October 20). Get rid of performance review! *Wall Street Journal.* Available at http://www.wsj.com/articles/SB122426318874844933.

Langer, E. (1989). *Mindfulness.* Cambridge, MA: Da Capo Press.

Osney Grange Group. (2009). *Agenda for change.* Available at http://www.brookes.ac.uk/aske/documents/OGG%20agenda%20for%20change.pdf.

Pink, D. (2011). *Drive: The surprising truth about what motivates us.* New York, NY: Riverhead Books.

Psychology Today. (2014, November 21). What is mindfulness? Available at https://www.psychologytoday.com/basics/mindfulness.

Sadler, D. R. (2013). Opening up feedback: Teaching learners to see. In S. Merry, M. Price, D. Carless, & M. Taras (Eds.), *Reconceptualising feedback in higher education: Developing dialogue with students* (pp. 54–63). London, UK and New York, NY: Routledge.

Stone, D. & Heen, S. (2014). *Thanks for the feedback: The science and art of receiving feedback well.* New York, NY: Penguin.

Vella, J. (2008). *On teaching and learning: Putting the principals and practices of dialogue education into action.* San Francisco, CA: Jossey-Bass.

Examining current practice and policies about feedback

Use this tool to identify supporting policies related to feedback and determine adjustments needed in those policies to create a system conducive to an effective feedback process.

a) Identify existing policies, guidance, procedures, etc. that incorporate the use of feedback associated with professional growth or learning.

b) Note if and how those policies define feedback, specify its purpose, identify responsibility, and establish the quality of feedback.

c) Based on the analysis, propose changes in existing policies, guidance, procedures, etc., needed to strengthen the feedback processes in practice.

Policy areas	Definition	Purpose	Responsibility	Quality

Author

Joellen Killion serves as senior advisor to Learning Forward, after serving as the association's deputy executive director for many years and as its president. She contributed to the development and implementation of state policy by creating and facilitating the use of practice guides in several states and in overseas, international, and American schools in multiple countries.

She is a frequent contributor to Learning Forward's publications. Her books include *What Works in the Middle, What Works in the Elementary Grades,* and *What Works in the High School, Teachers Who Learn Kids Who Achieve: A Look at Model Professional Development; Assessing Impact: Evaluating Staff Development, 2nd edition; Collaborative Professional Learning Teams in School and Beyond: A Tool Kit for New Jersey Educators; Taking the Lead: New Roles for Teacher and School-based Coaches; The Learning Educator: A New Era in Professional Learning; Becoming a Learning School;* and *Coaching Matters.*

She authored and co-authored numerous papers, reports and workbooks such as PDK's EDge, The Changing Face of Professional Development, and resources associated with the Transforming Professional Learning (TPL) initiative in Kentucky and six other states. TPL resources are available at www.learningforward.org/publications/implementing-common-core.

The creed Joellen lives by is:
Excellence can be achieved if you . . .
Care more than others think is wise . . .
Risk more than others think is safe . . .
Dream more than others think is practical . . .
Expect more than others think is possible . . .

Contact information:
Joellen Killion
Senior Advisor
Learning Forward
8 Prestonwood Circle
Lakeway, Texas 78734
joellen.killion@learningforward.org